Stansty

A story of the land and its people

Quentin Dodd

Stansty – a story of the land and its people
First published in Wales in 2010 on behalf of the author
by
Bridge Books
61 Park Avenue
WREXHAM
LL12 7AW

A CIP entry for this book is available from the British Library

ISBN 978-1-84494-069-1

Printed and bound by
Gutenberg Press Ltd
Malta

Contents

INTRODUCTION

This was a project started by my late brother, Keith, who as a surveyor set out to investigate the disappearance of a road at Stansty, for which he could find no explanation. This served to increase his interest and I, as the historian and lawyer, took over the project when he was taken ill. We continued together to find out why things had happened. I have pursued the project since his death.

When my father went to the auction in 1953 and bought Stansty without any consultation with my mother, it could have been thought to be getting off on the wrong foot. But we all grew to love living at Stansty and what it represented.

Stansty, in many ways, is a very ordinary piece of land. We are not even dealing with the whole township. The people who have lived there were important, even locally, in their time and give us an overview of how things developed. The Thompson family were rich in controversy and interest and, as far as I am aware, no attempt has ever been made to make an assessment of them. Little is known of Richard beyond his building of the cathedral in Wrexham. John was a charismatic, flamboyant and colourful character. One always feels sorry for the Victorian woman and those in the Thompson family are no exception. It is my regret that I have found neither painting nor photograph of any member of the Thompson family. I suspect that Richard was too gloomy and John was not still long enough.

This book is an attempt to chronicle two thousand years in the life of Stansty. There are inevitable gaps. I found the research interesting and I hope that you will also. I have tried to avoid pure speculation, but sometimes two and two do make four! I hope my reader will accept it on this basis.

In a project of this nature, help received from any source is much appreciated. Inevitably distance became a factor. I therefore acknowledge with very grateful thanks the help I have received from all local Archive services in Chester, Denbighshire, Flintshire and Wrexham and other local

6

studies centres. But more was needed and I must acknowledge the help from Margaret Watson at the Bodleian Law Library, Patria McWalter from Galway Archives and Mary Guinan Darmody at Tipperary Archives. I am indebted to my friend Brian Lowens for his photography.

I dedicate this book to my late brother, Keith, who started the whole project by his inquisitiveness and his persistent refusal to give up.

Quentin Dodd

Chapter 1
Where did it all start?

If you are writing about a piece of land and the events that are directly or indirectly connected to it, this must be a fair question. Stansty is first and foremost a piece of land. It is situated on rising ground on the north-west of Wrexham. It is essentially a well-drained area of good farmland with a gravel base. Up till the end of the nineteenth century, the four neighbouring farms if not run as a co-operative were run with the co-operation of all the farmers.

Land will leave evidence for the archaeologist but little for the historian. We can go back as far as Roman times, but little is known. In 1807, a Roman bath was discovered in Wrexham but was covered up again and no record of the site kept. We know the Romans were at Holt, and when the excavations were being made for Homebase, on what had been Plas Coch Farm, evidence was found of Roman occupation, but this appears to have been a brewery or distribution centre.

What became the Stansty township was land of a similar nature. Saxon Wrexham was a fact but little evidenced. When the Doomsday Book was produced, it ignored the Wrexham area. Gerald of Wales in his book of a journey around Wales chose to go directly from Basingwerk Abbey, Holywell to Chester. But life will have continued uneventfully except for border clashes between the English and the Welsh.

The building of Valle Crucis Abbey in 1200 was a symptom of the growing stability of the area. On 22 July 1431, a charter granting part of the township of Stansty to the abbey was made at Stansty and the original is in the British Museum. Stansty Ucha already belonged to the abbey but Stansty Issa now formed part of the manor. It is described as a copy of an extent made in 1314.

Stansty becomes identifiable as an entity, when in 1254 an area that Palmer describes as equivalent to the Stansty Park of today, was given to the abbey by Gruffydd ap Madoc, Prince of Powys, and consolidated their ownership of the township. This remained so until the dissolution of the monasteries in 1536. However, Derek Pratt tells us:

Lands distant from the Abbey had been the first to pass from its control. Leases and exchanges relating to both Stansty Abbott and the adjacent township of Stansty Uchaf indicate that, while the former Grange was not originally leased en bloc, a substantial family, the Edwards, found itself in the position to stand the higher rents demanded by the Abbots of Valle Crucis and to ignore the great financial risk involved in attempting to farm an entire township or the greater part of it.

Between 1487 and 1507 they were able to enlarge upon and consolidate the numerous small-holdings which had come into their possession during the early years of Dafydd ap Ieaun's Abbacy so that by 1577 the family held the greater part of both Stansty Abbott and Stansty Uchaf along with a large slice of the adjacent township of Gwersyllt.

We shall hear a lot more about the Edwards family and for those dedicated genealogists, Palmer has produced a family tree in his *Townships* book. But we must differentiate between ownership and occupation.

On the dissolution of the monasteries, and Valle Crucis in particular (1537), Henry VIII leased Stansty to Sir William Pickering whose son was later given a lease for 66 years by Edward VI. He was a bachelor on his death in 1574, but his illegitimate daughter, Hester Puckington, inherited. On her death in 1592, her husband, Sir Edward Wooton, took over and died a baron in 1630 without issue. But the Edwards were still in occupation as they had been since 1317.

The ownership issue is clouded by the tenure of copyhold that afflicted the estate for a long time. The Edwards were secure in their occupation. Justice was dealt with by the manorial courts held regularly until well into the nineteenth century.

Where did the name STANSTY come from? It is a place name from Old English *stan* (stone paved, stone built) and Old English *stag* (path or narrow road or footpath or narrow road footpath, mountain track, cattle track and senata semella narrow path). When this name was given 1300 years ago did a well-used track sufficiently prominent and rare for a place to be named after it exist. This is the explanation I found for the name.

Our ancestors had good reason for the choice of sites where they built their houses. Stansty Ucha and Stansty Issa were within a quarter of a mile of each other. There are natural springs to be found at a point between them which would have supplied both houses. These springs now feed the lake with regular fresh water.

In 1577, David Edwards built Stansty Issa or Stansty Park as it is now known. There had been a house on the site before and the house he built was later extended. David was a farmer whilst there was another branch of the same family in commerce in Wrexham. The Meredith's of Plas Coch were cousins.

We should get away from a belief that all the Edwards family were wealthy. They were certainly very industrious, but even in 1635 when John Edwards died, his possessions had a value of only £95 and these included eleven cows, one bull and two heifers and calves. The furniture was worth £16. They were thrifty, some more so than others.

David Edwards' plaque.

There is a hearth plate behind a fireplace bearing the date 1620. The hey day of the family was in Stuart times. David's brother, John, after attending Christ-church College Oxford and Westminster School became court physician to King Charles I. Another brother, Johnathan, went to Jesus College, Oxford, became a fellow and ended up as Archdeacon of Londonderry by 1679.

In view of the fact that John Jones is the most notorious personage associated with Stansty we should perhaps dwell on his personal history. He was born in Merioneth in 1600 (the same year as Charles I whose death warrant he signed). What was his connection with Wrexham? David Davies of Harlech in 1914 provided us with a potted history in *Ardudwy ai Gwron*.

Lived a life of 60 years during a period which proved brimful of vicissitudes. He became one of Cromwell's principal leaders in the Civil War ending his career in the Tower of London.

Early in life he was sent to a school in Wrexham, where he remained after the completion of his studies. It is evident that Walter Caradoc, an evangelist, his tutor whose influence made a deep impression on Wales also considerably influenced John Jones. This Walter Caradoc had also as pupils Morgan Lloyd and Kavasor Powell two of the most notable Welshmen of the period. Wrexham at this period of history was an important Puritan stronghold. Whilst John Jones (still a young man) lived in Dyffryn Maelor he came into contact with several respectable religious families in the Wrexham district especially one wealthy family who lived in the mansion of Stansty near Wrexham.

The owner was John Edwards, son of David Edwards, who built Stansty. He had also been under the influence of a church in Wrexham, ministered by Morgan Lloyd already mentioned. John Edwards had a daughter named Margaret and according to various accounts deeply religious and one of the most beautiful maidens in Dyffryn Maelor. She married John Jones. In the course of time, with the issue of the marriage — a son and daughter they moved to Plas Ucha Dyffryn Eliseg, near Llangollen. Through his connection with the Stansty Family he became friendly with the Myddletons of Castell–y–Waen. The Stansty family brought their whole resources in framing a resolution from The Independents of Wrexham, under the leadership of Morgan Lloyd antagonistic to Cromwell assuming the title of Lord Protector. Colonel John Jones, through his marriage into the Stansty family, wielded considerable influence in Dyffryn Maelor, and that John Edwards Stansty and Kilhendref were related, and were foremost Puritans included amongst nonconformity of Wrexham and its neighbourhood, and were staunch supporters of the Parliament in the Civil War and were important in the Counsels of the Commons.

He corresponded regularly with Morgan Llwyd. He saw plenty of active service and on the Restoration in 1660, did not try to run away but placed his affairs in Wrexham in order and returned to London to be beheaded and then quartered.

His wife, Margaret, had died in Ireland on 19 November 1651. John Jones later married Oliver Cromwell's sister. Margaret's brother, John, who died in 1673, is said to have fought for Charles I and married the widow of a Lancashire loyalist, for whose claim on her first husband's estate (put up for sale by the Commonwealth), John Jones himself put in a word describing him, his nephew by marriage, 'as of a honest, harmless, sweet disposition.'

John Edwards further added to the estate till it embraced most of Stansty township and extended into that of Gwersyllt.

There has survived a survey made in 1707 of the township of Stansty Isa which sets out the topographical boundaries, identifying physical features as they were then. It is an interesting document in itself and for this reason amongst others, I thought to set it out in full. But it is written in a combination of Jacobean/Queen Anne English and is difficult to follow. You can, using the present landmarks, identify the boundaries it describes. The first issue it clarifies for me is when it identifies butts in the area of Stansty within the wall. When we went to Stansty, metal detectors were continually finding pistol shot and other articles and relics from the Civil War period. There was no record of any action closer than Holt. It was clearly an area of pistol and musket shooting practice. There are seven butts recorded.

The reference to Plas Coch gates means, I believe, that the chronicler thought that they were special. I have written about the origin of the Stansty gates elsewhere and they were older than Stansty Hall. Did Richard Thompson acquire these gates from Plas Coch for his new hall after he had bought it?

This description is very interesting for many reasons. It is still possible to believe that these boundaries can be generally identified now. He certainly bought Plas Coch in about 1830.

The area was clearly blessed with practice areas for pistol and musket practice. In 1711, John Edwards the Elder and John Edwards the Younger were involved in a dispute with a neighbour, Robert Hughes, and this

Plas Coch.

53° GEORGII III. *Cap.* 138.				2427
The SCHEDULE to which the foregoing Act refers.				
Where fituate.	Names of Tenements.	Names of Tenants,	Quantities.	Yearly Rents.
In the Parifhes of Wrexham and Gref-ford, in the County of Denbigh -	Stanfly Iffa and Stanfly Ucha - Together with the Tythes of Corn, Grain, and Hay arifing within the Townfhip of Stanfty, and the Tythe of Hay arifing within the Townfhip of Brough-ton, in the County of Denbigh.	William Edwards and Thomas Edwards -	269 1 0	578 10 0

Extract from the Act of Parliament (53rd Year of King George III) showing the entry for Stansty Issa and Ucha.

resulted in the transfer of a piece of land for five shillings. It looks like a matter of high principle and involved part of Stansty Ucha.

We should consider the position of the Edwards family. We have seen they were not all Puritans and by the eighteenth century were part of mainstream Anglicanism in the town. John Edwards was Church Warden 1712–14, Thomas Baker was warden 1661–62, and married Jane Edwards of Stansty in January 1662. Palmer tells us the Priory in Wrexham was owned and occupied by the Edwards family. Mary Edwards is buried in St Giles churchyard. Their cousins, the Merediths, also figured prominently in parochial life.

Moreover, in 1773, the farmers of Stansty township were in trouble for not using King's Mills mill to grind their corn. Squire Yorke insisted on his rights and judgement was obtained against the Stansty farmers who had to pay the costs of the action.

The importance of the Edwards family declines steadily until the last of the line, Peter Edwards, died in 1783. He died without heir but his will, bearing the date of 3 June 1778, refers to six children – John, Mary, Sarah, Catherine, Peter and Thomas. They all must have died before his death.

Stansty was in mortgage to Hill of Hawkstone, Shropshire. At his death in 1783, Hill was owed £146,136 by the landowners he had lent money to, including £44,000 by Sir Watkin Williams Wynn. Edwards' debt was £200

Facing page: Auction particulars for Stansty Issa and Ucha, 1813.

DESIRABLE AND VALUABLE

FREEHOLD ESTATES,

AND

TITHES.

TO BE

Sold by Auction,

AT THE

RED LION INN, IN THE TOWN OF WREXHAM,

IN THE COUNTY OF DENBIGH,

Upon the 27th day of May, 1813, at two in the afternoon,

(Unless disposed of in the mean time by private contract, of which due notice will be given,)

THE CAPITAL

MESSUAGES,

CALLED

STANSTY ISSA, AND STANSTY UCHA,

WITH COAL, AND OTHER MINERALS UNDER THE SAME ;

Situate in the Township of Stansty, and parish of Wrexham,

And in the Township of Gwersyllt, in the parish of Gresford, in the county of Denbigh ;

AND ALSO THE

TITHE OF CORN, GRAIN, AND HAY,

ARISING WITHIN THE SAID TOWNSHIP OF STANSTY ;

AND THE TITHE OF HAY, ALSO ARISING WITHIN THE TOWNSHIP OF BROUGHTON,

IN THE SAID PARISH OF WREXHAM ;

Now in the tenure or occupation of Mr. Wm. Edwards, and Mr. Thomas Edwards, or their undertenants.

AND ALSO

All that Farm House, and the several Fields or Parcels of Land,

CALLED

THE FIELD BELOW THE HOUSE,

ORCHARD CROFT, CAE PWLL, AND GREENFIELD,

Situate at Stansty, and in the parish of Wrexham aforesaid ;

IN THE FOLLOWING OR SUCH OTHER LOTS AS SHALL BE AGREED UPON,

AND SUBJECT TO THE FOLLOWING CONDITIONS.

.....STER PRINTED BY J. FLETCHER, FOREGATE-STREET.

plus interest. Peter Edwards borrowed a further £4,660 on 1 July 1780 from Hill.

Stansty then passed into the occupation of the side of the family engaged in commerce in Wrexham. But the freehold went to Sir Edward Lloyd and his estate is so complicated that an Act of Parliament (Cap 138 1813) is needed to unravel it. It is described as:

> An Act for vesting certain estates devised by the will of Sir Edward Lloyd Baronet deceased in Trustees to be sold and for laying out the money to arise by such sale in the purchase of other estates to be settled under the direction of the Court of Chancery to the same issues.

His son was the first Lord Mostyn and a descendant, Bishop Mostyn, figures in our story a century later. But there is a bond between Stansty and the Edwards family. So in the auction following the Act of Parliament in November 1813, two of the commercial Edwards, William and Peter, who are in occupation, buy four lots for almost £12,000. However, they have to pay interest on the purchase price, as they fail to pay all the purchase money until May 1815.

Stansty Ucha (at 126 acres) and Stansty Issa (at 142 acres) were substantial in a township of 1811 acres. Crispin starts to appear as a name in the area and we have the Crispin or Crispinianna as names within the Stansty boundary. Saint Crispin is the patron saint of shoemakers and we find many of the properties are occupied by shoemakers such as Joseph Forgham who is in the Tollbar Cottage on the turnpike road. The frequency of Crispin makes one question whether there was a guild or society of shoemakers in Wrexham.

There was a growing industrialisation in Wrexham as the eighteenth century came to a close. Wilkinson had created his iron foundries and made use of local coal. Once started, the Industrial Revolution continued at a pace. The area attracted enterprising men and one of these who would directly affect Stansty was John Thompson, a Wigan entrepreneur who, with his brother James, took a lease on the Ponciau Ironworks in 1813. His son, Richard, who was still at school later joined him and they both remain operating for the next forty years.

The agrarian phase comes to a close and Stansty passes into the ownership of industrialists who keep it free from development, but amass a great fortune from their enterprises. John Thompson was a man of enormous energy and we can learn of him in the next chapter.

Chapter 2
John Thompson

The Industrialist

It is at this stage that John Thompson comes into our story. He never lived at Stansty but he would have visited his son there from time to time.

He was a native of Wigan and a charismatic and enigmatic character. He was born on 2 July 1772, but came to the Wrexham area in 1813 at the age of 41, to work the Ponciau Ironworks. The lease was for 25 years at a rental of £300 per year and royalties. There was a condition that all coal had to be bought from the landlord's collieries. He worked it until 1829 (16 years of his 25-year term).

John was one of three sons of James Thompson and his wife, Helen. The others were James, who was in partnership with John, and Richard who became a Roman Catholic priest. Their business in Wigan was as ironmongers and dealers and the business survived until the Second World War. It appears that the father, James, was a convert to Roman Catholicism and throughout the Thompson family, there is a varying degree of militant Catholicism.

It is not clear why John came to Wrexham as there were extensive coal deposits in the Wigan area and ironworks, but the coal was owned by the Earl of Balcarres who had made the personal decision to work it himself.

John married Margaret Bullock on 3 February 1797 at All Saints Anglican church in Wigan after a service in the Catholic church, and Richard was their surviving son. There was at least one daughter, as we shall see later, but the paucity and absence of any Catholic records does not help to clarify the family tree.

John and James took a lease on the Brymbo Ironworks in 1818 (which had been established by John Wilkinson) and John worked it until 1828. He had taken a lease in 1824 on the Ffrwd Ironworks and his firing of the first blast furnace was a popular event locally. Penson, the local road surveyor, was instructed to build a new bridge at Furnace in Frood in 1828 to help service

The remains of the wall of the blacksmith's shop at the Ffrwd Ironworks.

it. Indeed, the *Wrexham Guardian* in April 1871 felt able to report quoting a correspondent who knew John Thompson well:

> To give the history of the Ffrwd Ironworks and Colliery, in the main would be to give the history of a gentleman who has passed away from amongst us, now nearly twenty years. But the colliery was of an earlier date than the gentleman we allude to and was in part opened towards the end of the last century.
>
> About the year 1801, a number of gentlemen united in partnership with the intention of making iron at the Ffrwd, but they proceeded no further with their objective than the laying of a foundation for a blast furnace, on account of the coal seams, which had been opened in preparation for the works, being reported dangerous from the quantity of gas evolved. After this, the works lay dormant until about the year 1824, when the late Mr Thompson entered upon them. Prior to this date, Mr Thompson had been actively engaged in the iron and coal trade, in the neighbourhood of Wrexham, having from the year 1813 held the lease of the Ponkey Ironworks and Colliery, and in 1819 he added the Brymbo Ironworks and Colliery (£1500 per year rent), that he held for a term of ten years; and in the management of them he proved himself an able successor to the late John Wilkinson.
>
> Penycoed Pits were originally situated near Penycoed farm in Brymbo and

in 1820 were worked by John Wilkinson's trustees for John Thompson who now held the Brymbo coal seams and the lower which contained some workable seams, including the noted 'Queens Coal'.

In the year 1824, Mr Thompson succeeded to the lease of what is now known as the Westminster mines which embraced an area of 554 acres of coal and ironstone mines. He was also lessee of the mines under the lands of the late Mr Sergeant Atcherley, adjoining the Ffrwd. These, with other minor takes, furnished Mr Thompson with unlimited material for the manufacture of pig iron, with the addition of a larger coal trade.

Mr John Thompson was no ordinary business man, as may be judged by the fact that he carried on, at one and the same time, the Ponkey Ironworks and Colliery, the Brymbo Iron Works and Colliery and the Ffrwd Iron Works and Colliery. He failed to get the lease of Ponkey Iron Works renewed, and when his term in the Brymbo Works expired, he devoted his whole energy to the extension of the Ffrwd Iron Works and Colliery, and the site of the Ironworks eventually became his own freehold.

Here he produced pig iron, a brand that was in great demand, so much so that it was not an unusual thing for orders for the cold blast iron made there to be accompanied with cash on account, to secure their prompt execution. Mr Thompson spared no expense in order to have his works at Ffrwd complete, so far as completeness was then known. The coal raised at the Ffrwd Colliery was of good quality, very suitable for the manufacture of pig iron, and the seam known as the Main coal was in great demand. For a long time, the City of Chester was supplied with gas made from this seam, and the town of Wrexham for a time was also lighted by gas made from the same coal. When the railway was extended to the works, the demand for this coal exceeded the supply; although at times, the pits were kept at work day and night to try to meet the demand, a state that continued during Mr Thompson's lifetime.

This ignored his continuing interests in Wigan. A correspondent in 1827 commented on John Thompson:

The public spirited and wealthy individual being at present the sole lessee of three great concerns in the neighbour hood, viz Ffrwd, Ponkey, and Brymbo furnaces, is perhaps the most extensive iron-master throughout the United Kingdom. He employs in these and in his other engagements, upwards of a thousand hands, thereby diffusing subsistence and comfort to no less probably than five thousand persons — It has long been the fashion to eulogise titled characters, and those of large landed estates or influence: but it would be a difficult task to point out the man who confers such real, permanent, and widely extended benefits to his country, as Mr Thompson.

These wide and extensive claims were too much for another correspondent who wrote on the 15 February 1827:

I was very much amused at the want of knowledge betrayed by one of your correspondents of the 9th February last in stating that John Thompson was perhaps one of the most extensive Ironmasters throughout the United Kingdom. Now really it appears to me your correspondent wished to merely administer a dose of fulsome flattery, which could never by any chance be gulphed down by the wealthy individual in question.

He goes on to give statistics for Alderman Thompson, Guests and Crawshays in South Wales suggesting a sevenfold discrepancy.

I do not at all wish to depreciate Mr Thompson's liberality, but merely the liberality of your correspondent, who wishes to give Mr Thompson more of the Iron Trade than Mr Thompson is aware he possesses.

We should try and bring this argument into perspective. The making of pig iron in North Wales in 1825 was 13,100 tons rising to 25,168 in 1828. In 1839, there were thirteen blast furnaces in operation in North Wales producing 33,800 tons. This was more tonnage than many parts of Great Britain at that time. It is very clear that throughout this period, John Thompson was a very substantial contributor to that total.

John Thompson was one of those trying to promote the Trent Valley Extension and Holyhead Railway as a director. This was in late 1846. Records showed Thompson paid most royalties in North Wales. There is evidence that fair competition meant over-bidding another.

I told him that we were very much hurt at his allowing Mr Thompson to step in between us and Mr West.

The original correspondent was trying to convey the importance he attributed to John Thompson. His activities have been poorly recorded. He represents the period between Wilkinson and the expansion of Brymbo in the second half of the nineteenth century. He provides that link in a period when

Facing: Map of the Ffrwd Ironworks.

19

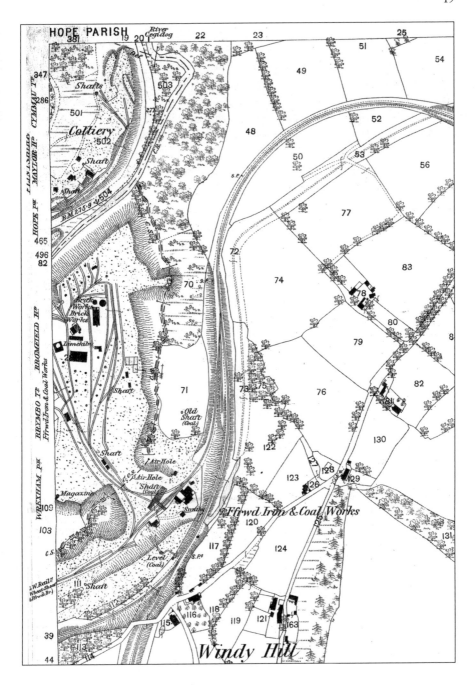

Wrexham was embracing the Industrial Revolution. Thompson's importance has been grossly underestimated.

Ffrwd Ironworks was open until 1903 and was a large producer. Very little is left now. Even the slag heaps were removed during the Second World War to aid runway construction.

John also took a lease on the Summerhill pits in 1824.

It is interesting to consider the working conditions in the collieries as described to the commissioner inquiring into the state of education as reported by the *Wrexham Registrar* in 1848. These are the comments of the Reverend W. G. Davies, perpetual curate of Brymbo, to that Commission.

Children are employed as early as 8 years of age in the coal-pits, but not for hard work: their average age at which they are employed is 12. Many have large families, and when the eldest boy reaches 12 years of age he is sent to earn something towards the support of the family. At this age a boy can earn 8d per day, and in a short while as much as 14d. Many of the men employed in the collieries are given to drink, and the mothers send their boys to work in the hope of securing some money to replace that which their husbands squander in the alehouse. With proper management and economy, the children might be left at school instead of being sent to the pits at 12 years old. A short time ago, perhaps, it might have been difficult to maintain a family without the assistance of the children: but wages are better now: for the last twelve months they have been as high as 2s9d per day. Great numbers of young women are employed at Brymbo to work on the banks: They are fond of the employment, because it brings good wages: They earn 1s a day by it. It is too hard work for any woman to perform. It consists of clearing the wagons of masses of coal and iron ore and removing these masses from the mouth of the pit. There is scarcely a pit to be seen without women working together with the men and working, quite as hard. They are necessarily thrown together with men in a promiscuous manner, and occupy the same small huts together with the men. This mode of life has an injurious effect on the morals of the women

But we must not let ourselves run away with the idea that John, after moving to Ponciau, centred all his industrial interests in the Wrexham area. He was certainly interested in railway developments in other parts of the country such as Cheltenham and Oxford. This was the railway over which he sued Gandell and Bruton in 1846.

He and his son, Richard, are again in the Chancery Court in a case relating

The Ffrwd Ironworks, c.1890.

to a colliery in Wigan that continues after John's death and that of his brother James. The case involved many parties and on 4 July 1853, the section of the judgement concerning Richard and John was an order:

> An account of what is due to the said defendant Richard Thompson for principal and interest upon such security and in relating the said accounts all just allowances were to be made to all parties and in that case it was ordered that the said taxing master do tax the said defendant Richard Thompson his costs of this trial including the costs of the said John Thompson deceased and it is also ordered that the said mortgaged be sold.

This must have been a bonus for Richard as the Thompsons were not used to being successful in court.

It is rapidly becoming apparent that John Thompson is a figure of considerable regional significance. But we have nothing to record his achievements. It is ironic that a Clayton Road exists but not a Thompson Road.

The Employer

By the standards of the time, John Thompson treated his men well. He had taken over the Ffrwd works and invested heavily. In late January 1827, the blast furnace was ready for use. The *Chester Chronicle* of 9 February tells us:

> On Saturday week, the worthy and opulent proprietor of the Ffrwd Iron works, Mr John Thompson to celebrate the commencement of their operations, or as it is technically termed, 'blowing in' gave to his workmen a grand treat upon the occasion. At six o'clock on the previous Friday evening, a well fed ox was set down by the fire in due form, and at two p.m. on the following day the 'lads of hard metal' in numbers about four hundred, were regaled with the 'Roast beef of old England' thoroughly washed down with copious liberations of 'Crwu da': and after comfortably enjoying themselves until dark, they all retired peaceably in good order to their respective homes.

In 1843, a Methodist chapel was built at Ffrwd, adjoining the site of the works. It would be difficult to accept that John Thompson did not make a substantial contribution to the building costs. Is this the chapel that Edward Watkin had been to on 4 October 1850 concerning which we shall learn more?

In January 1847, he pays the fine and expenses imposed on an employee, David Jones, for driving one of his coal carts on the turnpike road without his name being painted on the side. It was really the responsibility of the employer, but other employees had let him down.

There was a Friendly Society that bore his name and survived long after his death. In 1892, it cancelled its AGM on the grounds of cost (a dinner for all was involved). At that time, it had 205 members and over £700 in the bank. There was a tea being given to junior members in the Golden Lion Hotel, Coedpoeth on 17 January 1896, and it survived until the 1950s as we have a membership card from that date. It was clearly affiliated to the Order of Oddfellows.

But his major support for his men is seen in the incident known as the Bryn Mally riot. He inspired loyalty in his men that he fully reciprocated. Although in his late seventies, he was always getting involved in new projects. In 1849, he bought the freehold of the colliery of which Thomas Clayton, a young twenty-three year old, originally from Chorley, was the lessee of the Coed-y-Brain shafts of the Bryn Mally pit.

We do not have to rely on the newspapers alone for this story as the defendant's solicitors file in the subsequent assize trial has survived. The

No. 110 Bro T.E Lloyd						
LOYAL						
JOHN THOMPSON LODGE						
No. 1684						
Established 1839						
Independent Order of Oddfellows						
Manchester Unity Deeside District						
Lodge Room:						
PENYGELLI JUNIOR SCHOOL, COEDPOETH						
KENNETH HUGHES, Secretary,						
17 Linden Avenue, Hightown, Wrexham.						
Star Press, Coedpoeth. Tel. 250.						

T.E Lloyd.

| Arrears end of 1953.................... | | | No. 110 | | | |
| War Con.......... Monthly Con.......... | | | Total Con. 2-0 6 | | | |

Lod. Night 1954	Contri. due	Paid	I.C.B. Con.	Fines	Levy	Sec.'s Signature
Jan.	1					
Jan.	29	#/1	Card			
Feb.	26	2-0L			2/-	
Mar.	26	2-0L				
April	23	2-0				
May	21					
June	18*	4-/				
July	16	2-0L				
Aug.	13	2/0				
Sept.	10	2/0				
Oct.	8					
Nov.	5	4/1				
Dec.	3	2-0				
Dec.	31*	2/0				

* Clearance Nights.   Fine of 1/- for not clearing.

An example of a membership card for the Loyal John Thompson Lodge, 1954.

defence explanation was that the freehold property was purchased by John Thompson, including Coed-y-Brain pit, on 28 June 1849. By the conditions of sale at that date, he was to be in receipt of the rents from 1 November and took actual possession on 2 February 1850.

Clayton had been working the pit up to 31 October when he abandoned working and took away all the old rails from the pit bank, telling Mr Thompson he could not work the coal to a profit. Thompson having no work for some of his colliers who had worked out the coal from one of his pits, put up a whimsy on 1 March to get the coal out of Coed-y-Brain that Clayton had abandoned four months earlier. Clayton having heard that Thompson had prepared to work the shaft by erecting a whimsy and gin called to see him. Thompson showed him the lease that required that if the work at Coed-y-Brain was suspended for more than a month, the lease was forfeited. Clayton seemed satisfied by this explanation. Thompson could take possession and had done so.

On 3 March, Thompson saw Clayton and reminded him of the provisions of the lease. This was after Clayton had learnt that Thompson had erected a whimsy and a gin. He then claimed he knew nothing about the matter. The contrast between the attitude of the two men as employers is startling.

Thompson wanted to keep his men working whereas Clayton would only do so if he made a profit. They would not have been paid if they had not been working.

On Sunday, 3 March 1850, John Jones, a hammer man employed by Mr Barlow at Gwersyllt Ironworks, called to see Mr Thompson at his home, Sunnymede in Cefn-y-Bedd, at about six o'clock to say he wished to communicate some information to him in private.

He had been in a public house that evening with George Fisher, a workman employed by Clayton who told him that Clayton had given his men notice to be at his colliery, Bryn Mally, at 12 o'clock that night to load coal but he knew that it was to go from Bryn Mally to Coed-y-Brain to pull down Thompson's whimsy and machinery. Between one and two o'clock in the morning of 4 March, Robert Edwards and William Williams called at Cefn-y-Bedd and from his bedroom window told Thompson that Mr Clayton's men were pulling down the whimsy and machinery and breaking it. They asked for instructions.

Thompson told them not to molest a single man and to do nothing but take their names down and he said the same to some of his other men. Hugh Edwards, a man employed by Clayton, said that Clayton's bailiff, Ellison, had told him they were coming to the Ffrwd for a fight. It is also alleged that several of Clayton's men would give evidence of this once they had secured alternative employment. They were dissatisfied with Clayton who had brought men from Lancashire to work which threatened their jobs.

Edward Watkin was Thompson's manager and clearly a God-fearing man and unlikely to be a natural rioter. He would have said that on returning from chapel that Sunday, David Williams, one of Thompson's labourers, was waiting for him at the house door and told him that the Bryn Mally men were going to take down Mr Thompson's whimsy at Coed-y-Brain.

> He suggested I sent two or three men to watch. About ten o'clock, three men were in position to protect their master's property. At about 1 o'clock, a messenger said they had started to take down his whimsy. I went with pencil and paper to put the men's names down and was engaged in going from one to another for this purpose.

Thompson's men were peaceably obstructing and observing Clayton's men taking the whimsy down and a fight broke out. When it became apparent that Clayton's men would not succeed, Ellison, who was in charge of Clayton's men, sent for the police. The police took sides with Ellison in spite of Watkin saying to them that they should be there to keep the peace.

One of Thompson's employees alleged that one of the constables, O'Donnell, pointed his pistol (provided providentially by Clayton!) and threatened to 'blow your brains out' during the fighting. They did not fire and eventually parted the factions and arrested Watkin and one of the Williams' taking them with them.

Before the magistrates on a prosecution instigated by Clayton on 11 March Watkin, David Williams and William Williams were charged with riot and assault on Frederick Hutchinson, Clayton's bookkeeper. The evidence heard from Clayton's men was that 'they had been set upon by Thompson's men.' Understandably, it was a *cause celebre* in the neighbourhood. The three men were committed for trial at the Denbighshire Assizes on bail that was set at £200 for each, with two sureties of £100.

I have no doubt that John Thompson provided the funds. The bail was high and bail itself was unusual for such charges at that time.

On 1 April, the case came up in Ruthin but was stopped after only one witness of seven employed by Clayton had been heard. In the defence brief, the evidence for the prosecution is described as:

from what Mr Thompson knew of his own knowledge and what he is hourly hearing from his own men and Mr Clayton's own men he can prove all the witnesses to have perjured themselves, if Mr Clayton dared to swear what he thought what would prove his case why not do so but to employ men to perjure themselves, some of Mr Clayton's men have informed Mr Thompson's men that so soon as they can get work elsewhere they will come forward to prove the contrary of what Hutchinson, Ellison, Taylor and the Irish Policeman has shown.

Although the committal proceedings had taken two to three days, the magistrates had clearly made a terrible mistake failing to accept the use of reasonable force to protect property, as the wrong defendants were before the court. After the acquittal they tried to justify their decision. In all the papers they had published the following notice:

Having been the Magistrates before whom the case Regina v Watkin and others for riot and assault was investigated at Wrexham, we consider it due to ourselves as administrators of justice in the locality, and to the clerk of the sessions our legal and responsible adviser, to declare, that after an anxious and unwearied examination into the merits of the charge during three distinct days we came to the decision, that consistent with our sense of duty to the public and to the maintenance of good order we had no alternative but to send the parties accused to take their trial at the Assizes.

It is, therefore with no small degree of surprise that we learn of the throwing out of the indictment by the Grand Jury at Ruthin on Monday last after the examination of one witness only, there being at the same time the names of seven others, whose testimony was of no ordinary length and importance, indorsed on the bill.

In the view we adopted, we have the satisfaction to find that we are fully borne out by the opinion of an eminent and experienced Counsel, now leader of the circuit, as the accompanying document will show; and we feel called upon, in consequence of the importance of the case as regards the peace of the neighbourhood, to justify the course we feel it our duty to pursue in the matter to the public as well as the inhabitants of that locality which is the usual sphere of our magisterial duties. Lord Dungannon and W.H. Smith.

They also misunderstand the counsel's opinion. He more or less says that if you believe everything the witnesses say you can commit, but then goes on to say:

> But as the Grand Jury only examined the first witness, as one of so many, and the Judge had suggested that a civil right might possibly be in question, I can readily understand how they came to ignore the bill.

They were clearly hanging magistrates, not prepared to contemplate perjury or the law. They could not accept that they had been duped. It is perhaps ironic that the next press report after the committal proceedings reports a mine fatality at Pendwll Colliery at Moss, operated by Clayton, where a rope lowering the miners snapped and seven were killed, falling about sixty feet. It is easy to appreciate the preferable employer so far as the men were concerned.

That Edward Watkin was an upright citizen is perhaps confirmed by a report in the press in December 1850 that his house had been burgled and a small amount of money stolen while he was in chapel.

Thompson possessed so many good qualities, which can be put into one expression 'as a generosity of spirit', and it is a pity that his son Richard was unable to inherit them.

The Litigant

Richard inherited from the Thompson side and from his wife's Irish parents, the love of litigation as a recreation. John thrived on it and first crossed swords with the turnpike authorities and their wish to improve the road system around Wrexham. This was in 1831 and the cost of his coal would have been increased by the charges. He had obstructed the highway and the Quarter Sessions had supported him.

He employed Allington Hughes as the solicitor for his Wrexham area legal work, whilst for work in the Wigan area, it was Gaskell. We have a copy of an Allington Hughes account of money due and received on his behalf at the time of his sudden death of £1,184-0-6. It is a running account detailed from 1840 until his death and shows his involvement in commercial matters when he was over seventy years of age. The question of his involvement in the Wrexham, Nantwich and Crewe Junction Railway is dealt with elsewhere.

In 1846, he is involved in several cases in the High Court and the County Court. He sues Gandell and Brunton, the railway engineers, in relation to the Cheltenham and Oxford Railway. This was separate from the Sibson case. He also goes to arbitration in a dispute over the bridge at Gwersyllt.

He starts an action against the Trevor-Ropers of Plas Têg for specific performance of a contract. He loses, and on 1 April 1850, has to pay the defendant's costs of £260-16-4. But Trevor-Roper had been declared bankrupt in February 1848. The correspondence on the file is noticeably in Richard's handwriting.

John Thompson falls out with his racehorse trainer, Billington, and is sued for training fees. He loses and pays £111-13-9 in costs and the arbitration award. He has not paid the blacksmith, George Naylor, a further £18 who Billington employed to shoe Thompson's horses.

He is involved in 1843 in proceedings with a Mr Hackett. He is not a good neighbour and ends up in court at the behest of one of the Edwards family. Three cows and a calf belonging to Edwards had strayed onto Thompson's land. He kept them. It appears that both parties had some obligation to fence but Thompson had to be sued before Edwards could get his cattle back. It seems that there was a curious anomaly in that if common land was bought, no responsibility was on the buyer to fence what he had bought. So John Thompson's defence was that Edwards should have fenced. He argued ministry always took covenant to fence.

Dr.	John Thompson Esq, Wigan	on account			
1840 January 31	To amount of my Bill as per particulars delivered		68	9	7
1841 July 22	To Cash remitted Allen Roberts and Jno Jones Mold costs yours				
1843	At the suit of Edward Jones		9	18	8
Dec 27	To cash paid Willm Williams for hire & convey				
1844	Witnesses from Pulford against Hackett		"	10	"
June 17	To do paid Thomas Roberts Saddler expenses paid by him in conveying Witnesses against Hackett before the Magistrates in Decr last		"	6	9
March 25	To do paid David Williams Labourer on account of his attendance at Ruthin	18 6			
	To do paid Thomas Roberts Saddler	18 6			
	To do paid Edward Watkin	18 6			
	To do paid Robert Edwards	18 6			
1845	To do paid Thomas Walton	18 6	4	12	6
Feby 15	To do paid Edward Watkin (talana) for his attendance at Ruthin by your Sons request		"	13	2
	To do paid Thomas Roberts for do		"	13	2
	To do paid Robert Edwards for do		"	13	2
March 1	To do paid David Williams		"	12	2
3	To do paid Constables		"	10	"
1846	To do paid into Court yourself at to Darling		1	6	"
May 1	To do paid taxed Costs on Plaintiff accepting amount		6	1	4
"	Paid for order to remit		"	1	"
Feb 2	To cash paid Mr Wm Jones Jobt Wrexham Debt and Costs yourself at the suit after the Minck Bank		7	"	"
31	To do paid Messrs Morgan Pierce and Johnson assignee of Mr George Lewis Surgeon balance of purchase money for House and premises in Hope St Wrexham		747	"	"
1847 Jany 25	To do paid Fine and expences imposed upon your Servant David Jones for driving a Cart belonging to you upon the Turnpike Road without your name being painted thereon		"	11	"
	Carried forward		878	15	6

Part of the bill from solicitor Allington Hughes.

He bought a horse in part exchange from Stretch of Croes Newydd and then alleged it was not sound. Thompson returned the horse. The vet, Lees, supported him.

But the major surprise in the account from Allington Hughes is that most of the credits are of money being received from his son, Richard. The impression is left that John is an old-fashioned, cash only, entrepreneur.

The Man

He was in many senses an enigma. At the end of his life, he was living at Cefn-y-Bedd (when in Wales) with one servant, Ann Powell (25), to look after him. But he was still very much involved in affairs in Wigan. His home there was in Wallgate. He continued as senior partner in the family business of Thompson and Co in Millgate, iron merchants. At his death, he was an alderman of the Borough Council and the oldest member of that council. He remained a fierce Tory until his death. He was therefore in the last thirty years of his life commuting regularly between Wrexham and Wigan. Even though the coming of the railways in the 1840s meant it was less time-consuming, it was still a tiring journey, particularly for a man who was eighty-three years old at his death and agile enough to supervise his businesses from on horseback. His reserves of energy are truly amazing and one perhaps now understands Clayton's grave misjudgement.

We do not have many instances of his writing having survived. What we do have shows it to be very limited in style. This compares dramatically with that of his son, Richard, who had a flowing hand. Indeed in later years, he appears as a correspondent on behalf of his father.

John was a Tory and was involved in Lancashire politics in the pre-secret ballot days. There is a record of his speaking in support of Henry Greenall in 1837 in the West Lancashire constituency. His speech he had printed by Albion Press by Thomas Painter, a Wrexham printer. In his speech, he complained that the Whigs under 'Lord Melbourne, Lord John & Co' had brought the country to ruin:

> let me tell you in my business of manufacturing iron there has been a great depression by Lord Melbourne's misrule, as there has been in the spinning and weaving trades.

This election was at a time when the ballot was not secret and when fruit and other missiles were thrown by the opposition at the candidates and their

A sample of John Thompson's handwriting.

supporters. Greenall was not elected.

He was clearly convivial company. He would attend dinners in Wrexham where he would chair and/or speak. Such were the Catholic dinners for the opening of the first chapel, and his granddaughters wedding. His son was conspicuous by his absence.

Let us quote the views of a man who knew him, writing in 1871.

> John Thompson was generally to be found talking to a collier about the quantity of coal that had been raised the preceding week, in deep conversation with a furnace man about his last casting of pig iron, or giving directions to a groom about the training of a horse he had entered for the Gold Cup at Wrexham.

He even had a horse called Stansty that ran in the St Leger. Predictor ran in the Wrexham Cup in 1828 and Minerva and Orthodox ran at the same meeting. Heddibrae and Fenelon were to race at Chester on another occasion. Ostrich, a four-year-old ran in the Gentlemen's Subscription Purse and Town Subscription Plate in Oswestry in 1824. He had a stud, but the highlight of his racing career was winning the Newton Cup with his horse, Fitz-Dieter, which caused great excitement in the town of Wigan.

Perhaps this is a moment to pause and consider the horse's name. He only had one daughter Ellen and she married Adam Fitzadam in 1821 and who was in 1828 to become the Recorder of Wigan. He was a Protestant and his children were brought up as such, but the natural tolerance of John shows up here and also in the naming of his horse. His eldest grandson, John Thompson Fitzadam, started with him in the business but in 1859 read for the bar and in turn came to be Recorder of Wigan.

The *Chester Courant* reports in 1852

MELANCHOLY ACCIDENT AT MINERA NEAR WREXHAM
It is our painful duty this week to record the death of John Thompson Esq, ironmaster, of Wigan, Lancashire, and of Cefn-y-Bedd , near Wrexham. Mr Thompson met with his death under the following circumstances:- The deceased was riding his pony up the Ruthin Turnpike road, where there is a crossing of the Minera Branch of the Shrewsbury and Chester Railway to the Limekilns and Rocks, and whilst so, his pony was knocked down by the buffers of the engine and rolled over the deceased. He was immediately removed to the Miners Arms Minera when the assistance of three medical men was very shortly obtained but the deceased's injuries were of such a serious nature that he only survived about six hours, and never recovered his consciousness. He was a gentleman highly respected and in his 83rd year. He was the oldest ironmaster in the kingdom, having been in business for about half a century; and during his partial residence in this locality has carried on the Ponkey and Brymbo Iron works and latterly the Frood only besides works in Flintshire and Wigan. He was much beloved by his workmen, and upon his death being made known many poor families who were dependant upon him felt it more keenly than it is possible to imagine. The deceased is to be interred in the family vault at Wigan, on Saturday next.

He was killed crossing his own railway in Minera on horseback. He died as he lived, active to the last, an immensely popular figure. His body was taken back to Wigan to be interred in St Mary's Catholic Chapel there. He had been crossing the line to go and inspect his horses.

His son, Richard, was a very different person although he had some of his characteristics. Particularly, he will be seen to have his father's determination but in his case, this could manifest itself as a lack of sensitivity or over zealousness. We will now consider and study the complexities of Richard's character.

Chapter 3
Introducing Richard Thompson

He is such a central character in this story that we should try to understand him. He was born in Wigan on 15 July 1799, the only son of John Thompson and his wife Margaret, née Bullock, whom he had married on 3 February 1797 at All Saints, Wigan by license. Richard Junior was baptized by his uncle and namesake, Father Richard Thompson, John Thompson's brother. Father Thompson was undoubtedly a strong personality and in later years when he disagreed with a colleague he was certainly prepared to express himself forcefully in a doctrinal argument carried on by way of pamphlets. He was the rector at St Gregory's in Chorley for almost forty years, being responsible for building the church at Weld Bank in 1813 and its enlargement in 1829. This connection may have been the reason that our Richard withdrew to Weld Bank in 1855.

It is apparent that young Richard received a good education. At his funeral, Bishop Thomas John Brown, who gave the eulogy, is in some reports described as his superior, in another as his mentor, and in yet another as his friend. An examination of the career of Bishop Thomas John Brown shows his only possible contact to have been at school. By 1625, St Gregory's School and a Benedictine abbey had been established in Douai in France, populated for the most part by English monks. With the disturbed times in France with the Revolution, it was evident that Douai could no longer be relied upon to afford a home, nor could English parents be expected to risk the lives and liberties of their sons by sending them there for their education. If the work of the past was to be continued, it would have to be done elsewhere; and all hearts now turned with a great yearning to England. The pressure on Catholics had been reduced, although it was almost forty years more before Catholic emancipation.

At the beginning of 1795, permission was sought from the Committee of Public Safety that ruled France at that time to move the college, plus that at

St Omer, to England with all the masters and pupils. They crossed the Channel on 2 March 1795. An old boy of the school, Sir Edward Smythe, came to their rescue. An inheritance from his wife enabled him to offer the school a home at Acton Burnell Hall in Shropshire. He had seen the need for a home before they arrived and the hall was offered to them whilst they were still in France. They remained there until 1814 when they moved to Downside where they remain to this day.

They had few pupils at first, only six in 1798, in what is described as a sylvan retreat of Acton Burnell. By 1805, the number had risen to 17. Thomas John Brown, who was slightly older than our Richard Thompson, entered Acton Burnell in 1808 and moved with the school to Downside. He remained there until 1840, becoming an abbot. There are no records from Acton Burnell, but it is certain Richard did not move on to Downside. I believe there are good grounds for thinking they met there and started a life-long friendship. Additionally, it was at Douai that his Uncle Richard was educated.

At the age of 15 in 1814, Richard either did not feel any vocation or John, having only one son, wanted him home whatever his Uncle Richard wished. He remained all his life an unswerving Catholic, intolerant of any other faith.

Once home he joined his father in the business of iron-making, learning the intricacies and practices involved. We next hear of him running the Pant Ironworks at Rhosllanerchrugog in partnership with John Greenhow.

His Uncle James is in partnership with his father, John, at Ponkey but ceases to appear on documents, which now only carry John's name. I believe that Richard was involved although none of the papers that have survived refer to this being the case. There are however more and more property acquisitions by both men.

Richard meets Ellen Bourke and they marry on 18 October 1827 by Catholic rite in St Werburgh's Catholic Church, Chester and then go to St John's to legalise it by the civil law of the time. Richard describes himself on the marriage register as an 'ironmaster' while Ellen is a 'spinster'. This is interesting in itself as in *Pigott's Directory* for 1835, John is described as an 'ironmaster' while Richard is described as a 'gentleman'. Ellen's origins are dealt with in the next chapter. She was an only child, twenty-five years old while Richard was an only son, two years her senior.

The Catholic flock in Wrexham was still small but was increasing in number and Richard became the chief fundraiser in a campaign to provide a chapel to worship. We must remember that this was a time when the Church of England held political sway. Catholic emancipation had not taken place although there was an anticipation that it was coming. Similarly, the Nonconformists had not the equality they thought they were entitled to. We are dependent on the *Shrewsbury Chronicle* for a report of the event.

They tell us that until about 1820 there was only one Catholic in Wrexham. This is unlikely, but the conditions of the time meant that it was something the Catholics would keep to themselves. By December 1829, there were enough to merit their own place of worship. Richard bought some land in 1828 and the property was built in what was to become King Street.

Quarter Sessions records the certificate of the Reverend John Briggs of the City of Chester, Catholic Minister or Priest, that the newly erected room in New Street, Wrexham is intended to be occupied as a place or meeting of congregation or assembly for religious worship and for no other purpose, Easter 1828. The subterfuge of building the priest's house on the ground floor, with the chapel on the first floor, had to be carried out to deal with local opposition. The chapel was dedicated to St David on Tuesday, 17 December.

It is at this time we see, for the first time, the ruthless and aggressive streak in Richard. He does not deal with the opposition in the town to the building of the chapel by conciliation or negotiation. He simply tells the opposition that if they continue to oppose his building the chapel, he will build a blast furnace next to the Town Hall. There was no doubt this was not an idle threat.

The local Nonconformists had been generous in giving their support to Richard Thompson's financial appeal and were given a prominent place in the celebrations afterwards.

Whilst the Bishop celebrated High Mass, the Catholics had determined to put on a good show. The press went as far as to say this was unprecedented in the north of the principality since the Reformation. Tickets to attend cost 4 or 2 shillings: and amongst the music sung was a Mozart Mass, with a well-known soloist from within the Catholic hierarchy.

After the service, dinner was held for fifty people with the catering from the Eagles Hotel. Richard's father, John, presided but there is no record of Richard being present. The speeches reported do not mention him, nor do the toasts. The Liberal Protestants, led by Mr Griffiths of the Mount, were toasted in recognition of their financial contribution. The toast, proposed by Mr Griffiths on behalf of the Nonconformists, was 'The cause of Civil and

Religious Liberty all over the world' is perhaps indicative of the level of religious tolerance in Wrexham at that time. You will learn that this is not the only official occasion when Richard is unexpectedly absent. After the cathedral was completed, the St David's Chapel was used by the Baptists and, in more modern times, as a Kebab House.

The next event was the birth of his children on 11 November 1829 at Brymbo where the parents were then living. They were twins, John James Thompson and Mary Anne Thompson. Richard, after his marriage, was concentrating on building the home for himself and his wife and was engaged in land acquisitions to put together a block of land to site his hall on. Between 1830 and 1832, he built his house, described elsewhere, and set about providing for his privacy. In order to do this, he demolished Stansty Ucha manor house.

Quarter Sessions again tells us of his activities. In 1829, the Poor Law authorities for Minera fail to persuade Quarter Sessions that Richard Thompson should pay an assessment they had levied and the order is quashed. Again, although he had put together his block of land, there is still a public road that passed through this very close to his outbuildings. On 25 April 1831, he was allowed to divert this road further away from his buildings but the new route was still close.

On 13 May 1839, his mother-in-law died and in her will, which does not mention her daughter, Ellen Thompson, she leaves her entire estate to her son-in-law, Richard:

> all my estate holding and interest of in and to the Lands of Killoran in the County of Tipperary and also all my Real and personal property of whatever nature or kind soever that I am possessed of or shall hereafter be entitled to in Ireland or elsewhere to my son-in-law Richard Thompson.

This will was written by Ellinor Bourke herself in February 1837, even though it was in very legal language and this may have come from her being married to a lawyer for twenty years. Killoran, a 1500 acre estate in Tipperary, features in the chapter about her early life, and Lady Ffrench still owned it in 1870.

We learn of John Thompson and his response to ideas for an extension of the turnpike in 1829, but there is a letter written to the clerk to the turnpike

Facing: Part of a pamphlet bringing the activities of Mr Penson to the attention of the Denbighshire Justices.

TO THE

JUSTICES OF THE PEACE,

FOR THE

COUNTY OF DENBIGH.

Gentlemen,

Mr. PENSON (*without the consent of his Co-Surveyor, and contrary to the wishes of all the Rate-Payers in the Township of Stansty*), is endeavouring to obtain the view and consent of two Justices of the Peace to widen and alter an Highway of the said Township, which leads *to his own house*, at an Enormous Expence to the Township; whereas, the Highways at Rhos-ddu, which are *more incommodious and many yards narrower* are to remain untouched. Mr. PENSON is *no rate-payer*, and the owner of *seven acres of land only* in the said Township.

WE, the undersigned Rate-Payers of the Township of Stansty, being considerably more than four-fifths of the Inhabitants of the said Township, do hereby agree not to pay more than two shillings and six pence in the pound, being the amount of Rate allowed in any one year for the repairs of Highways of the said Township. See 5 & 6 William cap. 50, sect. 29.

WE, the said Rate-payers, will also endeavour to prevent by legal proceedings, the Surveyors of the said Township from destroying the foot-ways, and from lowering and widening the Highways of the said Township, and from thus incurring such extravagant and unnecessary Expenditure on the said Township.

WE, the said Rate-payers, do most humbly request, that no Justice of the Peace will grant any order to the said Surveyors for the purchasing of Lands, for the widening or otherwise altering the said Highways, in these times of such great distress to Farmers and others, especially when such Highways have always been considered (even before Railways were established) sufficiently commodious and convenient for the use of the public.

WILLIAM JONES, Highfield, Stansty.
CHRISTOPHER BENTHAM, Rhos-ddu.
MARY KEWLEY, Stansty Lodge.
RICHARD THOMPSON, Stansty Hall.
MARY HAYES, Gwdwen.
JOHN HARRISON, Plasgoch.
THOMAS PRICE, Rhos-ddu.
GEORGE HIX SALLERY, Rhos-ddu
JOHN ELLIS, Rhos-ddu.
THOMAS DAVIES, Rhos-ddu.
WILLIAM SHORE, Rhos-ddu.
HARRIET MEADOWS, Rhos-ddu.

CHARLES WAINWRIGHT, Stansty.
JOSEPH EDWARDS, Crispin.
SARAH TENCH, Grand Stand.
RICHARD WORRALL, Chester-Street,
JOSEPH FLOATER.
H. W. TONKINS, Crispin Cottage.
MARY ISAACS, Stansty.
THOMAS WILLIAMS, Station,
JOHN COWLISHAW, Frood.
WILLIAM JONES OWENS.
JOHN DAVIES, Stansty.

PRINTED BY B. HUGHES AND SON, WREXHAM.

trustees, Mr Humberston of Chester, written by Richard on behalf of himself and his father on 18 September 1840.

> I write in confidence to inform you, there was a meeting at Mr Penson's house to oppose your getting an act for converting the Stansty Township Road into a Turnpike Road. I told Mr Penson at the meeting yesterday (two persons being present) that the greatest part of the intended new Turnpike Road was through my lands and I would not contribute one farthing towards any opposition which might be raised against it, nor would my father for it would be a serious injury to his colliery (belonging to the Marquis of Westminster) if any part of the Gwersyllt Township Road was converted into a Turnpike Road.
>
> I fancy you have nothing to fear from any opposition for no sum of money will, or can be raised to prevent you from obtaining that Act although it might be attempted. I hope you will not divulge the information I have imparted to any person.

This is perhaps one of the most curious surviving letters that Richard wrote. What was he up to? He posed as a public-minded whistle blower. The Thompson family attitude was so different from that of ten years earlier.

It can be interpreted as a very deliberate attempt to ingratiate himself with those in power locally. The extension was blocked by the mineral interests in the area and so did not go ahead. Was it Richard's profound dislike of Penson that brought about this response from him. Perhaps it was this co-operation that lead to his magistracy and the ignoring of his road closure four years later. It was surely more than disagreeing with Penson on principle.

By 1846, Richard remembered that the turnpike authorities have not for two years paid the rent for the Tollbar Cottage that housed their employee, and chased them for it. A milestone in his life occurs when, on 19 October 1841, he was appointed a magistrate. After an initial flurry, he does not seem to have sat very often. He is perhaps accepted and becomes 'respectable'. He soon learned that it was what you are rather than who you are, that counted.

By 1845, the road that crossed his land had disappeared and there is no record of any action at Quarter Sessions. My late brother, Keith, a surveyor, spent hours trying to ascertain what had happened but without success. There were two local road surveyors, one was Richard's tenant farmer, John Isaac, who lived at Stansty Old Hall (or Stansty Park), and Thomas Penson, who was married to the daughter of Kyrke of Gwersyllt Hall.

Stansty Hall, Aug.t 25.th 1848

Dear Sir, I think the memorandum
I have made respecting the encroach-
-ments on the Highways made by
Mr. [Pearson] [gothers], will assist you
in the case for the opinion of
Counsel. I will send you the Plans
also before the case is sent up, I
think Mr. [Jervis] & [Welsby's] opinions
will be best, we shall then secure
them, but do not send the case
up until I see it, I shall be from
home for a week or ten days, making
as short journies as possible. I from
Sir [Dear Sir] Yours truly
[R. Thompson]

Letter from Thompson about the bridge at Bangor-is-y-Coed. NO B-ON-DEE THEN.

In 1845, Isaac committed suicide, according to folklore we inherited, by riding his horse through the hall and into the lake in front of the house and drowning. The inquest verdict was 'Drowned himself whilst labouring under a fit of insanity.' He died on 4 June and the inquest was held the following day. His wife and son continued to farm Old Stansty Hall for several years more. What was the reason for his acute distress? We do not know and although we have a record of the names of the witnesses called at the inquest we do not have a copy of their testimony.

Thompson knew how to create pressure on Penson. Bangor-is-y-Coed bridge is the boundary between Flintshire and Denbighshire. When it needed repair both counties had to contribute. Thompson set out to try and prove that Penson had cheated the county. Why should there be a personal vendetta? In residence terms, he was a near neighbour. He got information from the Clerks of the Peace in Denbighshire and Flintshire, and then pursued the suppliers of materials for information.

Of Dempseys, timber merchants of Liverpool, he asked:

I will thank you to furnish me with a copy of the invoice of the American Baulks be purchased by Mr Penson the County Surveyor for the repairs of Bangor Bridge about August 1843.

Again,

31st January 1852. In your account of the expenses furnished me as incurred by John Roberts Dempseys for Timber £19-15. I will thank you to inform me if £33-19-6 was paid to Thomas Roberts solely for the labourer's wages and if all the timber was used for the repairs to that bridge. I also perceive in your accounts that £1-6-10 and £2-0-3 have been paid to Thomas Griffiths for repairs to Plas Maen Bridge. You must be aware that the damage to that bridge was caused by yourself as one of Mr Kyrke's in getting too near the Bridge on the maps of the bailiffs in possession and then repairs plus two more.

In 1850, we reach the antithesis of Richard's dislike of Penson. He is in dispute again with Penson, and his strong dislike is acknowledged by Thompson in the instructions to counsel. Thompson objected because Penson had appropriated part of the road when he built a wall around his own property. Having regard to Richard's history of encroachment on common, this is rich indeed.

Valle Crucis Abbey.

In papers submitted to counsel it was said,

Ever since the appointment of the two gentlemen Mr Penson who is not on friendly terms with Mr Thompson and acting in direct opposition to the wishes of his County Surveyor has commenced system of annoyance by destroying some portion of the footpath made by Mr Thompson and adding it to the highway also destroying the footpath leading to Mrs Isaac's farmhouse although the highway is more than twenty feet away.

Richard marshals the opposition and petitions Quarter Sessions. Sixteen different encroachments were for Penson's own benefit and a total of 1,644 square yards were involved – a whole third of an acre! Compare this with Richard's encroachments that are described in chapter 7.

Richard was interested in the establishment of the Wrexham Literary Institute and made donations to them from time to time. In November 1854, £5 is recorded in the *Wrexham Albion* newspaper for example. Its aim is to promote young men's learning.

We learn that for a day out, the Thompsons would visit Valle Crucis Abbey on a regular basis. This is shown by the abbey's visitor book. It is difficult to believe that Richard Thompson would have not made visits to St Winifred's Well at Holywell, but there are no records of this. He was never as 'hands on' as his father with his work and would have had plenty of leisure time.

Ireland features prominently in this story and it is now time we learn about Richard's obstinate nature as is shown in Irish litigation.

Chapter 4
The original Irish connection

Hugh Bourke was born in County Tipperary in the early 1780s. He came from a well-off Catholic family of good lineage. However we know little of these because of the paucity of the Roman Catholic records and the habit of the activists in the troubles after the First World War of keeping warm by burning what they regarded as English records!

Hugh went to England in 1794 where he was articled to a Notary Public, Wilson Forster, in the City of London. Was he related to the Forster who was his sister-in-law's legal adviser, of whom we shall learn more? He completed his training and was admitted to the Society of Scrivenors in 1800. On 29 July 1807, he was given the freedom of the Company of Scrivenors to practise by redemption. He could start to practise. In 1812/13, he was fined over his performance as steward and ceased to practise in 1819/20. He was never a member of the Company's committee. He did not practise in the City of London before 1807.

He went home to Ireland and married Ellinor Everard (the spelling of her Christian name varies and as a result, her early life is not traceable). Everard was descended from the Norman French meaning boar hard. A daughter Ellen was born in County Tipperary in 1802. Ellinor had inherited an estate at Killoran in Tipperary that then passed down the female line in some way. It may also have been theirs during certain lives but we have no real information other than what a judge will tell us later. I believe that they were cousins of some sort. In the true Irish tradition, it is clear that going to law within the family was not unknown and we will have full details of one such dispute. I believe that during these seven years, Hugh Bourke held some judicial appointment under the Crown in Tipperary.

They then left Ireland and Hugh commenced practice as a Notary Public in the City of London in 1807. He later practised from Gracechurch Street which was well known as a commercial area.

We then arrive at the Everard *cause celebre* where proceedings were commenced in 1819 when the case was entitled Forster v Everard and Bourke and, when heard in 1843, was Forster v Thompson. I have much sympathy with the plaintiff, the family solicitor, who had to wait some thirty years for payment of his bill, in fact until well after his death.

Forster was employed as her solicitor by Catherine Long Everard (née Fitzpatrick) from 1792 until her death in 1813. The outstanding legal bill of over £700 was in 1810 converted into a loan to her secured by a promissory note. We learn:

Report of cases in Chancery – Forster v. Thompson.

FORSTER _v._ THOMPSON.

1843.

June 3, 5.

CHARLES SULLIVAN FORSTER had been engaged as the solicitor and law agent of *Catherine Long Everard*, from the year 1792 until the period of her death, which occurred in the year 1813. Some time previously, there having been a considerable sum due to him for costs, exceeding the sum of 700*L*, *Catherine Long Everard* borrowed from *Charles Sullivan Forster* a sum of 77*l*. 0*s*. 4*d*., for which she gave her promissory note, bearing date the 26th of July, 1810, payable at six months.

A. B. being indebted to her law agent in a considerable sum for costs, and also on a promissory note, by her will ordered, in the first instance, her debts to be paid as soon as conveniently might be after her decease: she then devised her real estate to her brother, and directed "that all costs and charges which might be due to her law

Forster had been employed by *Catherine Long Everard* as her solicitor in several causes, and, amongst others, in a cause "agent" at the time of her decease, should be paid by her brother out of the rents of the real estate. *A. B.* died in 1813. From the year 1815, the executors of the testatrix and the devisee of the real estate resided abroad, out of the jurisdiction of the Court; but in the year 1816, the law agent was paid, under an order of Court, in one of the causes in which the costs were incurred, a sum of 289*l*. 8*s*. 4*d*., and subsequently the further sum of 100*l*., by the agent of the devisee of the real estate. In 1819, the law agent filed a bill against the executor of the testatrix, and also against the owners of the real estate, to recover the amount of his demands; but in consequence of the absence of the Defendants no subpœna was served. In 1828, the Plaintiff in that suit having died in the meantime, his executors, the present Plaintiffs, filed a bill of revivor; but the Defendants being still out of the jurisdiction, no subpœna was served. In 1838, a second bill of revivor was filed, and subpœnas were served upon the Defendants, by means of an order obtained under the Statute 4 & 5 Will. IV. c. 82, which had been enacted in the interval:—*Held*, that the real estate was charged with the amount of the promissory note as well as the costs.

Held also, that the bar of the Statute of Limitation was saved by the filing of the bills in 1819 and 1828.

---

that Forster had been employed by her in several causes and, amongst others in Everard v Draper relative to certain lands in the County of Tipperary called Killoran to which she was entitled under a lease for three lives, with a covenant for perpetual renewal.

She gave Killoran by her will to her brother James for life and then to her brother John for life.

In her will she stated:

and it is my will and desire, that all costs charges, and expenses, which are due to my law agent Charles Sullivan Forster, at the time of my decease be paid to him by my brother James out of the rents, issues and profits &c, of the said lands known as Killoran devised to him as aforesaid; and the testator appointed her brothers James and John her executors and residuary legatees.

Catherine Everard died on 12 May 1813 and her will was proved by her executors.

James moved to change the succession so that his sister Eleanor would inherit and he died in April 1816. Eleanor (Ellinor Bourke) was living in England at the time of his death and never returned to Ireland. John, Catherine's surviving executor, had left Ireland in 1815 to live on the Continent. He never returned to Ireland either and therefore remained beyond of the jurisdiction of the court.

In the course of the judgement, it was apparent that he felt his sister, Ellen Bourke, should pay Forster as she had the benefit of the rents of Killoran. He had been visited in Paris in 1827 by a witness and expressed this view.

Two small payments on account had been made before 1819 when on the 1st April Forster's patience gave way and he commenced proceedings against the surviving executor John Long Everard and Ellinor Bourke and her husband Hugh Bourke the Notary Public claiming a balance of £866:12:6d.

He was seeking payment out of the Estate of Catherine Long Everard by asking the court to carry out her express direction to pay him.

No proceedings were had under this bill, nor was there any sub poena served, in consequence, as it was stated of the three defendants being resident out of the jurisdiction.

Charles Forster died in 1825, and on 17 September 1828 his executors renewed his claim against John Long Everard and his sister Ellinor Bourke, her husband having died in 1822, and to put a charge on the estate of Killoran

46

Ellinor Bourkes will.

to secure the debt. They also pressed for a sale of part of Killoran to pay the debt.

The court delays of the time meant that nothing happened before the death of John Long Everard in 1838. Eleanor took a grant to his estate and the plaintiffs revived their action again on 24 December 1838. Ellinor acknowledged the proceedings and then died leaving her entire estate to her son-in-law, Richard Thompson. Ellen Thompson is not mentioned in the will in Ellinor's own handwriting, but it could be said that as Ellen's husband, he could take the pressure of the proceedings better.

Ellinor had to accept the proceedings as an Act, passed in about 1835, enabled a person to be served with proceedings outside the jurisdiction. We shall see that it is not the first time that the law gets ahead of Richard Thompson.

So in 1839, Richard Thompson duly proved his mother-in-law's will and also took a grant to John's estate and thus became in point of fact, the personal representative of both.

Richard then starts to wriggle on the legal hook and tries to plead the Statute of Limitations The court was quite happy that, as the action had started in 1819 and the defendants had been obstructing progress by staying out of the jurisdiction, this was a non-starter. Then he alleged that the original will had not charged the Killoran estate with the debt. The judgement of the court was clear.

The will in the present case commences with such a direction, and contains expressions abundantly sufficient to make the real estate liable to the payment of the debts of the testatrix. This of itself furnishes an answer to the defence of the Statute of Limitations, which is relied on by the Defendant. But independently of this, the proceedings in the cause are quite sufficient to save the bar of the Statute. The original Bill was filed in 1819. At the time of the demand of Forster, the party who is now represented by the Plaintiffs, was unaffected by the Statute: and ever since that time there has been a pending suit. It is true, that for several years after the filing of the original Bill no effectual proceedings were taken in that suit. But the Defendant here cannot fairly rely upon this as a defence; the reason of the delay originated with the then defendants, the parties whom the present Defendant Thompson, now represents.

They were absent from the country, out of the jurisdiction, and thereby evaded the service of the sub poena. Under the law as it then stood, the Plaintiffs had no remedy. They could not serve the defendant with process, and the Court will not permit a party thus to avail himself of his own default, and set up a defence springing out of his own wrong.

We then see that the barristers acting for Thompson tried to argue the impossible, citing obscure cases. The Lord Chancellor, in giving judgement, showed that he was not going to be confused by the arguments of Thompson's counsel.

This case is somewhat complicated but when once the facts are understood there is no great difficulty.

After picking his way through the facts he said,

Then comes the more important question, as to the basis of the demand. The costs which were of a considerable amount, were furnished and made subject of an account as far back as the year 1819; It is evident from the endorsement upon the account viewed in connexion with the payment of the £100, that it must have been in 1819.

In that account credit was taken for two particular sums, one of which was part of a fund, which had been drawn out in a particular cause, and the other was a payment by the agent of the debtor; these payments were not carried to any particular credit, they appear generally on the credit side; therefore, there is no question as to this demand upon the Statute of Limitations, for there is an acknowledgement of the debt, and a payment made by the debtor, generally, on account of what is due on foot of the entire demand, and not of any particular item,

There is nothing to shew that the Plaintiffs should not be have the benefit of that suit, which has been regularly kept alive ever since. Again, there is the bill of 1838, to which appearance has been entered, because the law had been altered in the meantime, and the Plaintiffs served the process of the court as they would have done, if the law had allowed at an earlier period, and this bill is now brought into being.

As he comes to the end of his judgement, the Lord Chancellor made it very clear how he viewed the conduct of Richard Thompson and his in-laws.

Now has there been any misconduct on the part of the Plaintiffs to take away their right? None whatever. I see much to blame in the conduct of the Defendants: they attempted to evade the payment of their just debts, by residing out of the jurisdiction.

The Plaintiffs sought to realize a fair demand, which the law allowed, but the Defendants set them at defiance; the merits, in my opinion are all on the side of the Plaintiffs, and there is no legal bar to their right.

Richard Thompson had slotted easily into the warring faction represented by his wife's family and the Lord Chancellor clearly saw him as a rogue seeking to avoid his responsibilities.

The subsequent deed showed that he had to pay £1,250 for his recalcitrance to two principled ladies who knew the justice of their cause. It

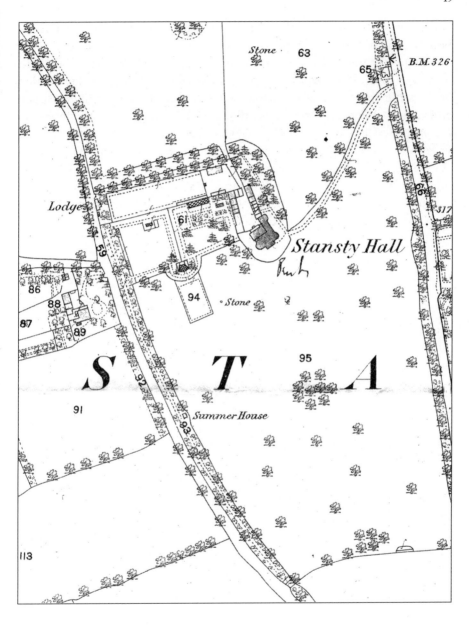

Ordnance Survey map, showing Stansty Hall and the gardens located between the Summerhill Road and the Mold Road.

had taken thirty years for Forster's family to recover his costs from the Bourkes and Richard Thompson.

The fate of the Killoran estate is interesting. It looks as though Richard may have given it to Mary Anne Thompson on her marriage, as her portion on the settlement. She was inevitably an absentee landlord by living in Dublin and Galway. We next learn about Killoran in 1870 from a statutory notice in *Freemans Weekly* calling for people who had a claim against the estate in Lady Ffrench's name to make it. The agitation of the Irish Land League had brought about in 1870 the first Act giving tenants a right to buy if they could afford to do so. There are no records of what happened to the estate.

But enough of Richard's pig-headedness, and let us now learn something of the home he built for his bride, Ellen Bourke – Stansty Hall.

Chapter 5
Richard Thompson's Hall

The period from 1820–40 is not renowned for its architecture. Very little is known of the building of Stansty Hall. We do not know either the architect or the builder. We have the lithograph of the period of Richard Thompson's occupation, but the only photographs to have survived were taken at a time when the hall had seen better days. We have the comments of Hubbard in his book: *Clwyd* in the *Buildings of Wales* series.

> Unremarkable stables remain. Also two columns which, being Greek Doric but with bases and enriched capitals suggest the house may have been interesting.

But he questions himself.

> But did they belong to the house? A lithograph shows it as chastely classical, long in proportion with a seven bay front and two curved bows. A four column porch on the return looks Ionic.

The lithograph that he refers to is one of only thirteen, in a limited edition, and few remain. It must be treated as an artist's impression, as an examination shows livestock could go up to the front door. There is no evidence of a ha-ha. He later kept longwool sheep and won prizes between 1843–47 at Denbigh and Flint Show.

We can observe the assembling of land by Richard Thompson to form an estate. Why he chose Stansty is unclear, but it was close to the town where he had organised the first Catholic worshipping centre. He selected a position on rising ground facing the town. Amongst his purchases had been Stansty Ucha farmhouse that he had demolished. He had money to build what he wanted. He also owned the Stansty Pound.

He did not deny himself of any facility that such a dwelling such as a hall should have. We do have the description of the house when he moved to Chorley in 1855 from that provided by the agents for the prospective tenants.

52

The lithograph 'Stansty Hall, Denbighshire, the seat of Richard Thompson, Esqr,' showing the view from the east.

The house had nine bedrooms. Downstairs, was a lofty entrance and staircase halls with a dining room, drawing room, music room, breakfast room, library and study. It had a servant's hall and butler's pantry, kitchen and excellent wine cellars. It had a force pump with excellent spring water for the use of the household kitchen and water closets. The garden lacked nothing.

The garden walls are all wired, and well stocked with fruit trees of the choicest sorts. The kitchen garden plots are also wired and planted with espaliers. Large Hot House conservatory pine and melon pits, cucumber frames etc.

How had the garden performed? We are told:

the hot-house contains some of the finest vines in the Kingdom, the fruit having several years obtained prizes at the London Horticultural Society Shows. The hot house pine and melon pits have just been re-glazed with large squares of the best double strong crown glass.

From what else did the Hall benefit?

This modern and commodious mansion replete with every convenience and suitable for a family of the first distinction, had out offices, stables, coach houses, harness room, clock room, fruit room, store rooms, milk house, cow houses, large sheep and cattle sheds, large tanks for the reception of rain and manure waters and every building necessary for a large establishment, shrubberies, walled gardens, pleasure grounds and park land enclosed by stone walls with young and thriving plantations. It is this wall of stone that still survives.

At that time, it was described as comprising 46 acres which is not very different from now. The Ordnance Survey of the time shows the layout including an ice house. Thompson was proud of his gates. He said they were magnificent and the entrance lodge handsome. He also claimed 'and is approached by a back lodge with handsome gates.' The final accolade was 'The Wrexham postman calls at the lodge with and for letters every morning and evening.' He wanted a tenant for at least fourteen years or more.

This description of 1855 shows that the property had obtained a maturity should have become more attractive with the advent of the railway, with the station being less than a mile away. Thompson had lived there since 1832 with his family but was now on his own. So he sold the furniture as well.

54

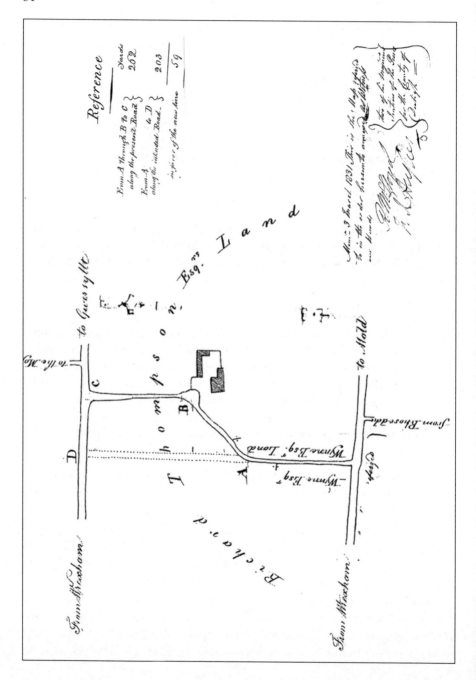

Facing: Plan of diverted road.
Below: The view from the house.

That meant virtually everything. The sale of the furniture at the hall took two days. From the coach house a (nearly new) chariot with rumble dickey cushions lamps etc as well as an excellent phaeton for one which runs remarkably easily and a capital gig.

What was the response to the 'To Let' advert? A tenant for fourteen years was found and we learn of his response to the perceived obligations to the people. The new occupier was Thomas Irven who is described in the 1861 Census as an oil merchant and drysalter. He was there for at least fourteen years. We do not know the rent payable. A drysalter, we are told, is a dealer in chemical products used in the art dyes etc and also in oils, sauces, pickles etc in the Oxford English Dictionary. He was as old as Thompson, being born in 1800 in Keswick in Cumberland. He lived at the Hall with his wife, Mary Ann, who was born in Surrey and his three daughters and two sons. They had a full complement of staff and their respective children. He had an orange tree in blossom in 1860.

He was still there in 1869 and we learn from the *Advertiser* in August 1867:

Annual treat at Stansty Hall Park – Yesterday (Friday) the Gwersyllt schools together with a number of their friends were most hospitably entertained by

Mr Irven in the beautiful park surrounding Stansty Hall, a treat which Mr Irven has made an annual one, and one always looked forward to with great interest by the juveniles who are the recipients of his bounty. A commodious tent erected for the accommodation of the guests in which 375 children sat down to tea accompanied by an abundance of buns, bun leaves preserves and butter. The elder guests including about a hundred of the toddlers, maiden aunts and other female relatives of the juveniles were supplied with a more substantial concomitants in the shape of seasoned boiled beef. The number of every grade who partook of Mr Irven's bounty was about five hundred. The fineness of the weather permitted the schoolchildren to enjoy themselves to the full in romps and gambols on the green sward; and in addition Mr Irven had secured the services of the eminent comic couple 'Punch & Judy' who had travelled all the way from Liverpool for the occasion. Punch was in excellent feather and Judy also acted her part well, and the numerous other personae of the play were so alive and the whole company being immensely amused by their efforts. The different diversions were kept up till the shade of evening set in when the little guests hied their way homewards with hearts filled with gratitude to the residents of Stansty Hall, Mr & Mrs Irven.

These copper beeches, which originally stood in the garden, were planted by Thompson.

The heated wall.

Although he was only a tenant, he clearly accepted that he should be part of the community and the new use of the Stansty Hall Park for the community is established under him. It is no longer a place of privacy.

At the end of his occupation about 1869/70, he moved to Oak Alyn, Cefn-y-Bedd and died in 1873. He sold land for the Wrexham – Connah's Quay Railway in 1871 for £780.

He was followed as tenant at Stansty Hall by Thomas Chilton and his family. He was there at the time of the 1871 Census but he had moved by 1882. He died in 1908 in Llandudno and his funeral and cremation were in Liverpool before his ashes were interred in Gresford. He was Chairman of the Bristol and Foreign Marine Insurance Co based in Liverpool. He is remarkable for having seven daughters and one son and only one of the daughters married. He was a Unitarian by faith and, on his death in 1908, left £67,000 and inevitably complicated provisions to look after his widow and his daughters, the youngest of whom was then 44. But for me he left an indelible mark! He organised a cricket match at Stansty against his own eleven.

After this, the house had caretaking staff and there are no records of any other occupiers – his staff had generally been from Ireland. It is said that the view of the nearest colliery (Rhosddu) was a detriment.

John Isaac's door at Stansty Park.

When we moved to Stansty in 1953, there was a rectangular piece of metal nailed up in one of the shippons with the words 'Lady Ffrench Stansty Hall' found on it. It has since been identified as a carriage plate. I have found no evidence of any visits to the Hall or indeed Wrexham by Lady Ffrench but why have a carriage if you cannot conceive using it.

The house remained empty until the start of the First World War when it was requisitioned for troops. There is no record of this in the Government papers at Kew but I have had second-hand reports of the way it was trashed by them. It is suggested that the Hall was demolished in 1920 but I think it was more likely to be 1924 when Dyke Dennis became the owner. Only part of the rear remains and this was attached to the stable block and is converted into a house. 1924 seems to be the date of demolition as by then there appeared at Stansty Park (Stansty Issa) several items that had previously been part of the fabric of Stansty Hall and gardens. The arch over the front door is now incorporated into the façade and there are large stone troughs and the gate that were part of the Hall installation. The arch does not appear on a photograph of Stansty Isaf (Park) when it was the Golf Club House.

Having decided to move, what does he do with the furniture? He clearly knows his son John will not return. He himself will not return. Lady Ffrench is living permanently in Ireland. So an auction is the only solution. At Stansty Hall on Friday and Saturday, 25 and 26 May 1855 starting at 10 a.m., Mr Edisbury the local auctioneer conducts the sale. Virtually everything in the house and outbuildings is sold. There were three hundred and sixty lots in all to be sold including 'a ladies exercising chair on springs.' He was moving into very limited accommodation as you will hear.

There is a curious rockwork folly in the area which would have been Richard's garden that no–one can explain.

However out of all the works done by Richard in creating his hall, we must single out the Stansty Gates and these are discussed in the next chapter.

Chapter 6
The Stansty Gates

It may come as a surprise to find a whole chapter given over to these, but there remains that air of mystery concerning them. When we have seen that Richard Thompson built his hall, he did not stint himself on what he provided for himself. He had two entrances to his hall, one each from the Mold Road and Summerhill Road. The Mold Road entrance was his main entrance and his drive swerving to the left to come up the front of the Hall. The gates and surround were expensive and beautiful as can be seen. These remained in place during his occupation and his daughter's ownership until her death in 1906.

There is speculation concerning the origin of the gates. The late Ifor Edwards suggests the gates may have been moved to Stansty from Erddig in 1772. I think this unlikely as the Edwards family who occupied Stansty Isa (Stansty Park) were not particularly financially successful and the wall into which they fitted so well was built by Richard Thompson himself who had laid out the boundaries. Certain gates did leave Erddig in 1772 but I do not believe they came to Stansty then.

Palmer tells us they were made at the Ruabon Foundry about 1832 and Thompson definitely erected the gates. But, with regard to the surround at the entrance, Starke Gardener referred to the railings 'the first existing richly worked with horizontal border forming the screen with modern gates.' It is not surprising that Simon Yorke of Erddig dearly coveted these gates and had done so for some time. Lady French had clearly been unwilling to sell but, when Bishop Mostyn inherited, his approach to the estate was very different. He used the estate as a source of capital for projects and in effect dismembered the inheritance. It was not until Dyke Dennis bought in 1924 that the estate was re-assembled so far as was possible. By this time, the main gates had gone.

I do not believe the gates came originally from Erddig to Stansty There

The main lodge (now known as Mollington with the Erddig gates in situ.

was no boundary into which to place them. Thompson had been buying extensively and I believe this included Plas Coch Hall described in 1675 as having nine hearths. The gates to Plas Coch are described in the Survey of 1707 in terms that cause you to think they were special. The gates now at Erddig are generally believed to be 18th century.

On 8 March 1907, Simon Yorke's agent W.N. Capper advises him that the estate trustees have made capital available to him and 'I have to inform you that the beautiful gates at Stansty are now for sale the price asked being £300.00.'

We then learn from the *North Wales Guardian* that, in July 1908, the gates were unveiled at the Marchwiel end of Forest Drive.

Interesting Ceremony at Erddig

There was an interesting little function at Erddig on Thursday last week, the occasion being the opening of the new gates at Sontley Lodge. The gates were unlocked by Master Yorke who rode through on a pony. The gates which are very valuable and of great historic interest were formally fixed on the Stansty

Hall Estate. Amongst those present were Mr & Mrs Yorke and Party, Mr Capper (Agent) and the employees of the estate. Mr Yorke complimented the workmen upon the admirable manner in which the work had been carried out after which the health of the heir was honoured and an excellent repast was partaken at the Hall. (*Wrexham Guardian* 31/07/08)

This prompted Simon Yorke to write in the next weekly edition an account of the restoration and his obvious pride in possessing them describing them as second only to Chirk, Leeswood Hall and Eaton Hall.

Erddig and the Stansty Gates
To the Editor

Sir, The little ceremony which has been so nicely described in your last weeks issue was in itself of so homely and private a nature that we had not thought it worthy of a place in your columns. As however you have done us the honour of recording it, may I be allowed to add a few remarks, and through this medium express the gratitude we feel towards the many kind friends who accorded us their good wishes and congratulations on that occasion – (a birthday); and for the valuable assistance of those through whose instrumentality I was enabled to purchase these beautiful gates, and transfer them from their former place at Stansty, where they had for generations been familiar to the public gaze, to the place where they now stand, at the Marchweil end of our Forest Drive.

First, I would mention that, through the obliging courtesy of the Rt Rev Dr Mostyn, Bishop of Menevia, I was enabled to negotiate for them, and to acquire them for a fully moderate price, the park which they had formerly graced the entrance to having been the property of the late Lady French, at whose death two years ago, it became the property of the Bishop.

The removal of the ponderous iron-work and the massive stone-work in which it was set, was effected by my Erddig staff of workmen, under the superintendence and most able direction of Mr W.N.Capper, the agent to this estate, and carried out in so masterly a manner that not a particle of damage was sustained by any portion of it, for which he is deserving of the very highest praise, especially when it is considered into how rusted and brittle a condition it had fallen owing to Stansty having for many years been without a resident owner.

Great portions of the elaborate ornamentation had in that long period of neglect became damaged, many pieces having been lost; those have however been clearly re-instated and copied from the original design by the skill and patience of Mr Joseph Wright, who for more than 20 years has been blacksmith to the estate; and all who had ever observed the fabric closely when in the former place will appreciate and admire the splendid manner in which the gates have now been restored to their ancient beauty and elegance, being now made by his art as good as new.

The setting up of them in their present position reflects also the greatest possible credit on Mr William Gittins, who for nearly a quarter of a century has been foreman to this estate, and who is so well known and highly respected throughout this district.

The Forest Drive is now adorned with an entrance second only to those of Chirk Castle, Eaton Hall, and Leeswood, which are too well-known to need any further mention here. These gates were made at Ruabon Foundry, according to my friend Mr A.N. Palmer, about the date 1832, at which time the art of iron working reached a very high degree of perfection, and nowhere more so than in and around this district. The name of the maker is, we believe unknown, but the excellence of his work will merit the very highest admiration of all beholders throughout generations to come as it has already done in the past; and we rejoice to think that these gates and their accompaniments should now occupy a position worthy of their magnificence, and of their handsome neighbours at the Coed y Glyn entrance, familiar to all and which with gratitude we remember as having been the kind gift of our tenants, friends and well wishers in and around Wrexham, on the happy occasion of our marriage in 1902.

Philip Yorke, Erddig, August 4th 1908 (Reprinted from the *North Wales Guardian* August 7th, 1908)

The gates were relocated by the National Trust to their present position at the end of the canal where the formal planning of the garden shows them to advantage.

There are still people that will argue that the gates were made by the renowned blacksmiths Davies Brothers of CroesFoel. I think this unlikely as if they had made all the gates claimed they would have had to lived twice as long.

But the story does not end there. The gates newly erected by Simon Yorke are claimed in 1910. We do not know the lady to whom he writes (it might well have been Ellen Margaret Ormiston) but her claim is treated with the utmost seriousness by Simon Yorke. We find he knocked Bishop Mostyn down in price and he is prepared to give her the gates on recovery of his outlay. But nothing more seems to have come of it.

Erddig Park, Wrexham, March 23 1910

My dear Madam

I am truly sorry to hear from you that the beautiful iron gates at the Sontley entrance to this Park, are an unlawful possession. I did not know anything about you and your claim to them at the time I purchased them from Lady French's trustees. The negotiations however, took so long a time that a claim had better have been made (as easily might) before the gates had actually been removed from Stansty; and even when they had been brought here, a long time was spent in the very necessary and extensive repairs to them, which had to be done by my blacksmith in the timber yard here.

Altogether, a whole year had elapsed between the time of my first negotiation and the setting of them up in their present place. Under these circumstances I do not think it would be a very easy matter to dispute my right to them; but by payment of the price of the purchase, £250 and the extra £30, which is the least at which I can put the cost of the repairs; & another £5 to compensate me for the cost I was put to in the removing of them and erection of them in their present place, you may have them without trouble of going to Law, assuming of course that you will also undertake the entire cost of their removal. With all the best respects to you I venture to think, my dear Madam, that this will be the best course, and one indeed which I shall be very glad that you should adopt; for I have a superstitious dislike to having any un-lawfully acquired possessions, (however innocently they may be acquired, so far as regards myself.)

With humblest apologies to you, dear Madam, for any trouble and annoyance to which my purchase of the gates may be putting you, believe me to remain very faithfully yours.

Ph Yorke.

Again if Philip Yorke had really believed that the gates had already been at Erddig would he not have said so, and been a lot less prepared to surrender them in 1910.

Richard Thompson would have had a gate at his lodge on the Summerhill Road as well. I think this gate was still there when Dyke Dennis bought in 1924. He took many articles associated with the Hall to Stansty Isa one of which I believe was this gate. He installed this at the boundary of the garden

Refurbished driveway gate from the rear entrance to Stansty Hall.

and drive. This gate with its surround is of the same age and we have recently had this gate completely refurbished by Mathew Hallett of Spurstow Smithy and it has regained its former glory.

But Richard Thompson accumulated his properties very rapidly and it is now time for us to learn how he did it.

Chapter 7
Department of Woods and Forests

This is the Victorian government department that was an anachronism. It had a wide range of duties and responsibilities that bore no relationship to each other. Amongst its responsibilities was cleaning the outside of the windows of Buckingham Palace. The nearest parallel in present times is perhaps Jim Hacker's Department of Administrative Affairs in *Yes Minister*.

The distinguished historian, Cecil Woodham-Smith described the department in her biography of Queen Victoria.

> The exterior of the Palace was the responsibility of the Office of Woods and Forests, a department noted for its dilatoriness: as a consequence the inside cleaning of the windows was done by the Lord Chamberlain's department, the outside by the Office of Woods and Forests. Thus, the amount of light admitted into the Palace depended on co-operation and good understanding between the Lord Chamberlain's office and the Office of Woods and Forests. If there should be a disagreement, the Queen must look at the world through obscured and dirty windows.

This department was also responsible for the protection of our Commons. With its reputation for poor performance and dilatoriness, it is not surprising that the unscrupulous took advantage. You could trespass on a common, build houses and get your money back in rents and more before the department took any action.

Richard Thompson knew how to work the system, and Brymbo Common and others were progressively 'colonised' by him. The office records at the National Archives at Kew show:

> Authorization for sale to Mr Thompson of the Crown Interests in certain encroachments in Brymbo Common Co Denbigh.
>
> After having considered your report dated 1 October 1842 and approving thereof these aree to authorise and require you to convey to Richard

I *Richard Thompson Esqre* of *Stansty Hall*
in the County of *Denbigh* do hereby contract and agree with the
Commissioners of Her Majesty's Woods, Forests, and Land Revenues,
to purchase the Interest of Her Majesty in a *twelve* Tenements or Parcels of
Land, containing *Nine* Acres,
Two Roods, *Eight* Perches,
or thereabouts, and lying and being at *Stansty and Gwersyllt*
in the Parish of *Wrexham*
being an encroachment within the Queen's Lordship or Manor of
Bromfield & Yale in the County of *Denbigh* for the Sum of
Twenty Nine Pounds *Eight*
Shillings, and ———————— Pence, (subject to the
usual reservation of Mines and Minerals, to the right of sporting over
the same, and to all other Royalties whatsoever, to Her Majesty).
And I do hereby request that the said Commissioners will grant me a
Conveyance of the said Parcel of Land on Payment of the said Sum of
Twenty Nine Pounds, *Eight*
Shillings, and ———————— Pence. And I do further agree
to pay annually on Michaelmas day, until the purchase is completed,
a Rent equal at least in amount to five per cent. on the Purchase
Money to the Receiver General of Crown Rents for the Principality of
Wales for the time being ; which said Rent became due and payable
from me at Michaelmas, in the Year of Our Lord One Thousand Eight
Hundred and *Thirty Seven*

Signed this *29th* day
of *January* One
Thousand Eight Hundred
and *Thirty eight*
in the presence of ————

Richd. Thompson

Richd. Oldfield
Samuel Bostock

Contract for purchase.

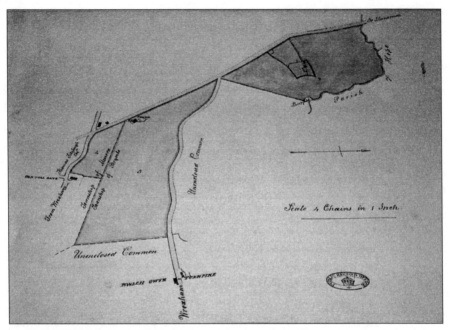

Map of Brymbo Common, 1860.

Thompson Esq, of Stansty Hall in the Parish of Wrexham Co Denbigh, in your said report named or to whom he shall nominate and to his, her or their heirs and assigns on payment in to the Bank of England in the usual manner of the sum of £114:8 received from him in the year 1833 and the sum of £10 recently remitted by him, making together the sum of £124:8, all the right title of her Majesty in and over severall parcels of land being encroachments made by him on a waste called Brymbo Common in the said parish of Wrexham containing in all 8a 1r 12p or thereabouts reserving to her Majesty, her heirs and successors all mines and minerals, the rights of sporting and their royalties over the same and also reserving the right of way to the Chapel and Pound (alluded to in your report) which are not to be included in the grant and likewise a well or watering place situate on the said land, the use of which has hitherto enjoyed the neighbouring freeholders together with the right of way thereto in which deed of conveyance you are to cause to be inserted such clauses as your solicitor may think necessary to prevent any claim of the purchaser to compensation, in the event of any dispute between him and the Commissioners in respect of the rights of the latter over the said land.

County of Denbigh
Lordship of Bromfield & Yale

List and Valuation of Encroachments at Stansty
and Gwersyllt in the Parish of Wrexham in the
possession of Richard Thompson Esqre of Stansty Hall
in the County of Denbigh –

Nos on Plans	Description		Quantity of Land A R P			Value at 7 years Purchase £ s d		
	Stansty							
1	Plantation	Lte of Wm Edwards	"	3	8	2	4	4
12	A Croft	Do Mary Salisbury	"	"	19	"	3	6
13	Cottage and Garden Do Do		"	"	1¾	6	2	6
14	A Croft	Do Do	"	"	20	"	17	6
15	do	Do Jno Ad Hes	"	1	"	1	15	"
20	Land called the Gorsey Piece		3	3	14	7	"	"
21	A Croft	Wm Thompson	"	1	16	2	9	"
23	do	Le of Saml Roberts	"	"	18	"	11	8
24	do	Lte of Mrs Rogers	"	1	6	"	14	"
25	do	do	"	"	22	"	14	"
27	do	do	"	"	13	"	3	6
	Gwersyllt							
A	Land	Lte of Thos Jones	3	1	15	6	13	"
			9	2	8	29	8	"

Agreement for the purchase of an encroachment, January 1838.

There is a letter about this written by the office to Richard Thompson on 1 July 1834.

I am instructed by the Commissioners of his Majesty's Woods to inform you that is has been found necessary to have the Wastes within the Lordships of Bromfield and Yale in the County of Denbigh resurveyed which will necessarily cause some delay in the completion of the Sales of the several Encroachments there but that so soon as that survey shall be received by the Board your Conveyance will be forthwith completed and forwarded to you.

But an earlier letter to Thompson's Accountant on 6 November 1833 reveals the sheer scale of Thompson's encroachments.

In answer to your letter of the 28th ultimo offering on behalf of Mr Thompson of Stansty Hall the sum of £93.10.0 for the purchase of 44a 1r 12p of land situate in the parish of Wrexham being at the rate of £2.0.0 an acre for 41a 3r 32p which amounts to the sum of £84.6.0 and 2a 1r 20p at £4.0.0 making the sum of £9.10.0 amounting together (as above) to the sum of £96.16.0 …

There are in the deeds notes appended to an Abstract (a list of the passage of the title or ownership) which further explain the scale of what was going on.

Is this a Conveyance of the Crown Rights in a number of the small properties purchased by Richard Thompson; cottages & small pieces of land a number of which it appears from the documents of title were originally enclosed & title acquired by adverse possession. 48 acres in Brymbo, Minera and Wrexham 8th November 1842.
31st Dec 1844 24 small pieces of land (on some of which houses stood) encroachments from Common in Townships of Gwersyllt, Stansty and Broughton. Reference is made to previous endorsement.
2a 2r 2p of land Bwlchgwyn in the parish of Wrexham bounded on the north by the Township road leading to Brymbo being an encroachment from Brymbo Common.

The figures do not all match and the period of the transaction was lengthy to say the least. I should at this stage refer to a meeting of landowners held at Mold in April 1838. They were protesting about the behaviour of the Office of Woods and Forests. It was not a well attended meeting.

The land owners [the *Chester Chronicle* tells us] were not called upon to resist the just and uniformly recognised rights of the Crown, but claims of a most inequitable character and which had only been heard since Mr Wilkins had been the acting agent. That gentleman was claiming and attempting to recover for the Crown all the wastes or unenclosed lands and was leasing minerals, the right to game, and in fact all other rights inherent in the freehold, though the property had been in the undisturbed possession of the owners of the adjacent land ... and in some circumstances where the landlord had, through the inconsiderable value of the property permitted the poor to enclose a few quillets and build a hovel, he had watched the occupant and let him be unmolested for twenty one years, which shut out the right of the adjacent landowner and then pouned upon the unfortunate industrious for the Crown.

Here was an official of the Office out in the field preventing the landowner acquiring Common land. His masters in London may have been incompetent but he was seeking to protect the position of the public and his department.

It is interesting to read later in the same report Trevor Roper of Plas Teg complaining:

that the land owners and cottagers in the neighbourhood of Hope were much harassed by these proceedings. For instance all the Crown rights, whatever they were imagined to be, attached to Coedpoeth, had been disposed of to Mr John Thompson of Minera; and the principle the Crown went on in such cases, was to lease everything but to explain nothing; but if Mr Thompson chose to proceed in the name of the Crown, where was the remedy?

The Thompsons recognised how the system worked and ruthlessly exploited it. The landowners thought they were still Barons in the time of King John.

Before you think I am being unfair about Richard Thompson there are records of his paying the same Office the respective sums for the same type of encroachment. But with the Office inefficiency this counted for nothing and it was easier for them to give in and earn for the Government Whig or Tory. In present times, we hear about cases where a neighbour has encroached a few feet or yards with surprising consequences. Thompson took 48 acres at a time.

But we now have to conside the financial scandal that was the railway building project.

Chapter 8
The Wrexham Nantwich & Crewe Junction Railway

The 1840s were the time of the Railway boom. It was a decade when the British public showed clearly they had not learned the lessons of the South Sea Bubble, 120 years earlier. The obvious fact that money did not grow on trees had failed to get through to the general public.

The Shrewsbury to Chester Railway was coming through Wrexham in 1845 and the General Station was opened in November of that year. Some schemes for new railways were a scam from the outset (such as drawing a straight line on a map) whilst others were the product of a fertile imagination. Some schemes failed because of the incompetence or inexperience of the promoters. It was a century and a half away from the concept of a feasibility study that would precede such a venture today. How this venture is judged, I will leave the reader to decide.

The stupidity of people's behaviour towards the railway speculation is not just a question of hindsight. There was plenty of advice and warning available. The *Times* editorial on 26 November 1845 said:

For some months gentlemen of a speculative turn have been indulging themselves in the amusing pastime of incurring unknown legal responsibilities on behalf of imaginary railways, Beginning by adopting, in the first instance, the character of promoters and appointing a person to act as their solicitor, they rendered themselves liable to all the legal responsibilities attached to promoters; who, by the interpretation clause of that act, are explained to be, every person acting by whatever name in the forming and establishing of a company at any period prior to the company obtaining a certificate of complete (not provisional) registration. Whether, therefore, a body of gentlemen have consented to be called Committee of Management Directors, Provisional Committee, Provisional Committee of Management,

Provisional Directors or by any other name, they are legally promoters. By appointing a person as their solicitor they have made him their agent and in all matters in any way consistent with the duty of such agent, a very wide field for action, they incur all the legal responsibilities into which he might lead them. To attempt to explain what these various responsibilities may amount to, would for us be hopeless, as it will be for Her Majesty's Courts of law and equity an overwhelming task.

Wrexham did not escape the fever. So it was that in September 1845 there appeared in the local press an advert for this railway and advancing the case for it to be built. It was described as being:

to connect the rich mineral districts of Ruabon, Brymbo, Minera, Ffrwd, Talwyrn, and North Wales with Crewe and the manufacturing districts of Cheshire, Staffordshire, Lancashire and Yorkshire.

It will afford the best and most direct communications from North Wales through Crewe to Manchester, Stockport, Macclesfield, Congleton, Sandbach, the Pottery District and Derby and the Eastern Ports of England.

Among the multifarious Railway schemes now before the public, the most legitimate, and also the most likely to yield a fair remunerative return on the outlay, are the transverse Railways projected with the object of applying the existing want of Railway transit across the country."

The advantages of this Railway will also be very great to a large and most important agricultural district now entirely destitute of Railway accommodation, and will afford the means of supplying it with coal and lime at one third of the present cost. The allotment of shares preference will be given to holders in the Manchester and Birmingham, Manchester and Birmingham Continuation, and North Wales Mineral Railways.

If we examine those railways that had been constructed or were in the course of construction at this time, these claims made in this prospectus simply do not stand up to close examination.

The notice is published on 23 September 1845 and is under the signatures of William Jones and J. Devereux Pugh described as joint solicitors to the company.

The published list of directors is, on paper, impressive and is twenty-six in total. Many with local mineral interests are included with John and Richard Thompson among those listed. Also included are Townsend Mainwaring, MP. The Worshipful Mayor of Macclesfield (without naming him) Duncan

James, Samuel Perrot of Liverpool, Sir Ralph Pendlebury of Stockport, and Standish Mott of Lincoln's Inn Fields, London. Where they have previous railway experience by way of directorship it is shown. Some were real railways while others were mere pipe dreams, such as the Trent Valley Continuation Railway on its way to the North Wales coast. How many of these men knew they were provisional directors?

A later report was lyrical about the industrial opportunities:

It is satisfactorily proved by the evidence of persons best qualified to give a correct opinion on the subject that the district of Wrexham (even exclusive of what may be called the Ruabon District) possesses inexhaustible supplies of Coal, Ironstone, Lime and Lead of the best quality; the extent of the coalfield is about six miles long by two broad and the limestone is of greater extent; the vertical sections of coal presents fourteen successive strata of Coal of which ten are workable; these strata forty six inches of coal to the cubit yard … there remain 18,817,920 tons of coal with a square mile value £35,400,904.

These were among some of the most extravagant claims made in support of this line, which was to run through Holt, Malpas and Nantwich to Crewe using the gap in the Cheshire hills.

Having regard to what we learn later of the survey of the route, it is perhaps not surprising that the investors became sceptical about the proposed line. Gandell & Bruton Engineers of Liverpool were to carry out the survey.

Who are the real promoters? It appears they were the two Wrexham solicitors named in the notice and another Thomas Edgeworth, was made chairman. Did people know that earlier in the year of 1845 he had gone into partnership with Pugh? He was later first Mayor of Wrexham who re-elected himself on his own casting vote!

The plans were lodged with the three Clerks of the Peace (there were no County Councils then) Denbighshire, Flintshire and Cheshire and can be inspected in the respective archive offices to this present day. Parliament we shall later learn never received notice of the application. The share capital of the company was to be £450,000 in £20 shares (22,500 in number). The importance of these figures will be learned later on.

Let us now recall the *Times* interpretation of the law at the time; about provisional directors signing the prospectus for example and look at one John Foulkes who wrote to the *Chester Courant* on 1 May 1846 protesting about his being drawn into the controversy.

Having with astonishment observed in the *Courant* of Yesterday the report of the committee appointed to investigate the accounts of the above Railway whereby Messrs Jones and Pugh the solicitors and myself are represented to be the first projectors of the company: I hereby distinctly deny that I ever in conjunction with Messrs Jones and Pugh or anyone else proposed the same or that I ever consented to become a provisional committee-Managing Director or Shareholder: on the contrary in September last Mr Pugh solicited my consent to act on the provisional committee which in the presence of a third party I declined.

In October following the first prospectus was issued wherein to my surprise my name appeared amongst others as one of the provisional committee. When I remonstrated with Mr Pugh thereon and he made no reply or excuse and said that a fresh prospectus should be issued in a few days omitting my name.

A second prospectus was accordingly issued as promised.

I therefore deem a duty to myself, and the shareholders to communicate the foregoing facts to them through the medium of your paper.

It was said in October 1845 by the promoters that no more shares should be applied for as they are fully subscribed on the 31st it is said that they might have to pass over respectable people!

Indeed when the later legal proceedings are commenced, Richard Thompson confirms he received the invitation but at a meeting with William Jones on 22 October, he declined to sign the consent.

When his name was not removed from the second prospectus he wrote to Jones and Pugh on 4 December and they confirmed that he had been deleted since he had refused to sign, he had ceased to have any connection. Neither he nor John Thompson asked for an allocation of shares. John signed at first but withdrew after only a few days. The promoters clearly had a very cavalier attitude to the niceties of the law and involved people without any semblance of agreement on their part.

What was happening we only learn later when at the Feathers Hotel Wrexham, there is a public meeting of the company shareholders called on 20 March 1846. There were many agitated and very annoyed shareholders present. As the *Courant* put it:

the looks of dissatisfaction which characterised the bona fide shareholders indicated very stormy proceedings.

Wrexham & Crewe
Mineral Railway

Sir

We beg to lay the enclosed Circular
before you which will fully explain
this project, & to offer you a seat at
the Board of Directors. We undertake
to indemnify those gentlemen who
become Provisional Directors of this
Railway from all costs & expenses
whatsoever. Mr. J. Thompson Mr.
J. Kyrke & Mr. J. Foulkes have
each accepted a seat at the Board

We are
Sir
your most obed' Serv'.

William Jones

J. Samuel Pugh

Sol's to the Company

R. Thompson, Esq
Stansty

Invitation to Richard Thompson to join the board of the Wrexham & Crewe Mineral Railway.

The Chairman of the Provision Committee, Thomas Edgeworth, was appointed to chair the meeting. He attempted to evict a Mr Buckton who came with the proxies of many shareholders. He failed. Mr Shaw of Huddersfield one of the Provisional Committee opposed attempts to evict him. A written report was then presented to the meeting on behalf of the committee. The Chairman started by stating the obvious:

He regretted it would not end in that in that satisfactory statement of financial matters which some time ago they had hoped would be the case.

The Provisional Committee had been placed in a position of peculiar difficulty, in consequence of the measures adopted against them by some of the parties they had employed. At the same time the Committee had felt it their duty to carry on their proceedings with the utmost economy, and with the most rigid regard to the interests of the shareholders; and he thought that no person, after hearing their statements would complain that they had made a profuse and wanton expenditures of the shareholders money.

It sounds as though there was worse to come and there was, as we shall learn. The report of the Committee was read to the meeting. After regretting the undertaking had not been successful they went on to say (below are a few extracts):

that the scheme was favourably received by the public is evidenced by the fact that between the 3rd October and the 24th of the same month, upwards of 150,000 shares were applied for and letters of allotment were at a premium before the scrip was issued, and there was every reason to believe that the sum of money required to be deposited with the Accountant- General would be immediately raised.

The Committee encouraged by the favourable reception which the undertaking met from the public, and bearing in mind that any delay would render it impossible to prepare the necessary documents for going to Parliament in the ensuing session and looking at the very large number of shares applied for, felt themselves called upon to proceed immediately with the surveys of the line and in taking any other measures for bringing the undertaking before Parliament at the earliest period. (A Parliamentary Bill had to pass through Parliament before a new Railway could be built and Parliament did not sit all the year round.)

Early in October last, an Allotment Committee was formed to whom was confided the allotment. The Committee, being determined to make a proper and equitable allotment of the shares, investigated every application, and forwarded letters of enquiry to any referee given by the applicant, in order to obtain a respectable and influential body of shareholders: and on the 24th of the same month, the Committee commenced allotting the shares, but in consequence of the number applied for greatly exceeding the number at their disposal, they were necessarily compelled to pass over the applications of many highly respectable persons and in nearly every case to allot only half the number of shares applied for.

In order to avoid the aversions cast on the directors of other lines of Railway, who had reserved shares to themselves, to the prejudice of applicants, your Committee came to the determination of allotting every share at their disposal, without any reservation to themselves, or to the officers of the Company.

Immediately after the shares had been allotted, the Bank restrictions took place; this it is well known, had the effect of causing a great depression in the money market, which affected indiscriminately every project then before the public. Such was the extent of the panic that, out of 22,500 shares allotted only 8782 were paid upon.

In consequence of the sudden depression in the money market, your Committee, acting upon the advice of influential and competent persons, hoping that this depression would be merely temporary and relying on the honour of the allottees to perform this express contract which they had entered into with the Directors resolved to extend the time for payment until the 10th January.

In the beginning of October last, the Engineers commenced the surveys, and every assistance, which they required, was rendered them by your Committee, and the officers of the Company to enable them to prepare the necessary documents required by the standing orders of Parliament. Your Committee amply supplied them with funds to carry on the work, so as to avoid any pretext on their part for the work not being done in proper time, or efficiently performed. Your Committee advanced them £2000 at various periods: although the last two payments were made with considerable hesitation and reluctance on the part of the Committee, Notwithstanding the many assurances given by the engineers to the solicitors that all the plans and sections would be ready in good time, the plans etc to be deposited at the Board of Trade were not delivered to the solicitors until 11 o'clock am; on Sunday the 30th November last; however, by the most strenuous exertions the plans were deposited at the Board of Trade in time.

The plans etc to be deposited with the respective Clerks of the Peace, were not received from the engineers until 7 o'clock the same evening; but, with great exertions the solicitors succeeded in depositing them at Chester, Mold and Ruthin in due time.(This is in the days before County Councils.) It was not without great difficulty the solicitors obtained from Messrs Gandell and Brunton the plans and sections necessary to deposit on 31st December, with the respective parish clerks, and at the Private Bill Office with the Clerks of the Parliament and it was not until 29th December that these documents were handed to the solicitors; Messrs Gandell and Brunton having up to the 29th December refused to deliver them up until a large payment was made to them.

Since the plans and sections have been lodged with the various public officers, your Committee have discovered that they have not been prepared in accordance with the standing orders of Parliament; and they regret to state, that had the bill been introduced into Parliament the errors in the plans were so palpable, and the whole so defective that the bill must unquestionably been thrown out by the Committee on Standing Orders. Having discovered many inaccuracies in the engineering and being threatened with powerful opposition from two companies, the North Wales Mineral, and the Shropshire Union and Railway Company, your Committee were at once convinced that their only course was to abandon all intentions of going to Parliament, with the plans and sections so greatly at variance with the forms prescribed by the Standing Orders.

Your Committee wish to state that the Solicitors had not the opportunity of examining the plans and sections, to ascertain their correctness and conformity with the standing orders, previously to their being deposited; otherwise the defects which, they now have to complain of, would have been discovered at a much earlier period, and much expense saved. Messrs Gandell and Brunton now claim a balance of £1763;9s from the Company and they have brought action against several members of the Committee for the recovery of this amount. The plans and sections have undergone a careful examination, by a scientific and practical engineer; from the numerous errors and inaccuracies which have been discovered therein, your Committee have determined to resist the exorbitant demand made by the Engineers, and are advised that the sum already paid to Messrs Gandell and Bruton is quite sufficient for the work done and performed by them.

Although your Committee regret that they have been compelled to abandon their intention of applying to the Legislature this session for an Act they are convinced that a Railway which holds out such lucrative prospects to the Shareholders, as proved by the traffic table and so imperatively called for by the locality, must be carried out.

There followed several acrimonious exchanges between the Chair and Mr Downs, Mr Buckton and other shareholders.

Mr Downs in supporting a resolution for a shareholders committee to investigate the company's affairs stated:

it was not his intention in the slightest degree to screen the Directors if anything wrong could be proved against them: on the contrary, he now told the Directors to their face, that if they had dealt unfairly with the shareholders they were responsible for every farthing of the money, and he would be the leader of any party united to maintain the rights of the share holders, He was aware what constituted criminality in a Railway Directory, and if necessary he would be prepared to maintain a suit in equity against them.

The meeting was to be reconvened in four weeks. Railway speculation was for capital gain and the excuse of the directors for not allocating themselves shares is very limp. We shall learn how the solicitors benefitted, without in any way risking their capital. It is not clear how many of the twenty-six provisional directors were present. It seems very few. What was the contract made with the engineers? Such a major expenditure by a fledging company should surely be for a fixed sum, and/or even in those days a written contract or at least an exchange of letters. The Chairman does not seek to plead breach of agreement by them, but merely their work is not fit for purpose. It is difficult to see how any money is due to them unless the arrangement was excessively vague.

The meeting reconvened a month later and again the *Courant* was present. They were not going to miss this. They knew a good story when they saw it. But this time we know that only three active directors were present – Thomas Edgeworth, Lewis and Poyser. It will not come as a surprise to you the reader to learn that the shareholders did not see the demise of this project in the same terms as the Directors and Promoters.

The report of the Shareholders Committee started with complaints that they had not received full co-operation from the Company Officers. They had asked for production of the minute book, allotment book and the letter book. The Solicitors refused they said on the instructions of the Directors whilst the Chairman says later it was the Solicitors who had advised that course.

Mr Downes leading for the shareholders refuses to accept the excuse of the directors that it was only the accounts they were investigating. In the discussions that took place, it was clear that the Chairman and the Solicitors were desperate to prevent these documents being produced. Both parties knew the matter was not going to stop there, with threats and counter threats as to what was going to happen when the case went to Chancery. The findings were read to the meeting.

The Committee appointed under the resolution have paid attention, in the first place, to the projection and promotion of the above company, and from the documents which have been laid before them, they find that the first projectors of the said company were Messrs Jones and Pugh the joint solicitors to the said company, and John Foulkes Esq, of Ashfield near Wrexham. (We have Foulkes' account in his letter to the Courant.) The promoters were John Thompson, Joseph Gilham, James Kyrke, Richard Thompson, Thomas Itchenor Watts, Joseph Bullock, Joseph Seed, George Lewis, John Overend, and Thomas Edgeworth who seem to have embarked on this scheme on the 24th September 1845.

When we examine later many aspects of this case it will become apparent that the Shareholders drew these conclusions from an inspection of the records of the company that must have been in a chaotic condition for these conclusions to have been drawn. The letter to Richard Thompson offering him a provisional directorship is dated September and refers to others Foulkes, Kyrke and John Thompson having already accepted. This hardly puts Richard Thompson in at the beginning and we must consider Foulkes' later claims.

The preliminary announcement was that the capital should be £450,000 in 22,500 shares of £20 each, with at first £2 2s 6d per share deposit, but which was afterwards altered to £2 2s per share, the solicitors finding that they had made a mistake in calculating the allowance by the Act of Parliament for preliminary expenses; another mistake from the Solicitors.

The first proceeding which the Committee see any necessity to report, is the appointment and registration of a solicitor to the company, which took place on the 4th October following, when William Jones of Wrexham was appointed by the signatures of George Lewis and Thomas Edgeworth, as two of the promoters of the said company.

The absence of the allotment book prevented them finding out how exactly the shares had been allocated and if the giving of priority as alleged by the Chairman a month before was true. The report then proceeds to analyse the expenditure incurred on behalf of the Company by the Directors and the Company Solicitors. They find financial mismanagement on a substantial scale.

They do learn that the proposal to launch this railway was germinated at a meeting on 14 July 1845 on which date Mr Foulkes and others had been present consulting about the 'best course for the construction of a line of Railway from Wrexham to Crewe.'

Although this was three months before the Company was floated, the Solicitors had charged the company £43 18s 6d and a further £19 6s 4d before the appointment of a company solicitor. Jones and Pugh then had claimed £1,142 15s 8d and had received a third of this. It does become clear the benefit to Jones and Pugh of not taking shares. Gandell and Brunton had claimed £3,762 9s 0d and had received £2,000 for a survey and plans that were not fit for purpose.

The Company is therefore still in debt £2349 6s 10d and the balance in hand is £4514 5s 0d leaving a surplus of £2164 18 2d equal to 16s 5d a share amongst those persons only who have signed the deed; but it is presumed there are about 1500 shares outstanding for which the deed has not yet been signed, which will reduce the dividend to about 10s 5d per share.

The charges for horse and gig hire, and expenses, also appear to be enormous.

There is a charge for subscribers' agreement and Parliamentary contract in Messrs Jones and Pugh's bill, and there is also a charge for the same in Mr Raimondi's bill. (he was a London Agent)

Also the Stamp duty on Subscribers contract and Parliamentary contract is charged in Messrs Jones and Pugh's bill and Mr Raimondi's bill; also the same for binding the four deeds.

There appear to have been an enormous expenditure and most exorbitant charges by the solicitors after 30 November, (viz the solicitors bills alone during this period alone amounts to £619 17s 11d). There could not then be the slightest chance (from the state of the money market and ruinous panic amongst all Railway matters) that this project could be successful in going forward to Parliament, and when compared with the expenditure in other branches of the affair. There seems to have been a race amongst the parties concerned as to who should spend the most money, or in other words who should have the greatest slice out of the funds (although small in amount) then in hand. The wasteful extravagance of the whole of the parties is in the opinion of the Committee almost without parallel in the very worst of the Railway bubbles with which the autumn of the last year was so pregnant.

Upon calling for some authority given by the Directors to the solicitors for their expenditure, they said that they had no authority in writing in the minute book, and added that their instructions from the Directors were not to produce the minute book nor to make any statement to the Committee from the minute book.

Jones and Pugh incurred the expense of their own individual London agents. £1,018 14s 7d was spent after 30 November. The only members of the list of Provisional Directors who had shares were:

Townsend Mainwaring, MP 5	Richard Gough 1
Sir Ralph Pendlebury 1	Robert Johnson 1
John Rowbotham 5	Samuel Kenrick 15
John Buckley Johnson 10	James Kyrke 5
Joseph Bullock 5	George Lewis 1
Thomas Byrom 10	G.McDermott 5
William Byrom 10	Chas Poyser 5
James Dundas 20	Joseph Shaw 5
Thomas Edgeworth 30	Thomas Watts 5
Joseph Gilham 20	

The share allocation was hardly a ringing endorsement to the future of the Company from the Directors.

The Chairman admitted that only three directors had taken any part in the Company. Mr Buckton made probably the most memorable comment – they were awaiting proposals from the Directors, 'At present it was a game of single wicket – there were only three Directors to bowl at.'

The meeting ended in disarray, as the shareholders realized they had been the subject to one of the biggest rip-offs in Wrexham's commercial history. The directors were told in no uncertain terms that this was not the end of it.

Matthew Sibson was a tenant of a field on the proposed route and the Headmaster of Grove Park School. He does not feature in the *Courant's* reports of the shareholders' meetings. He was allotted forty-five shares. He was either the chosen vehicle for the shareholders action against the directors or he took it upon himself to spearhead the court action against them. Anyone in touching distance became involved.

So the case of Sibson v Edgeworth and others was born. The pleadings in the case are available at the National Archives. They consist of about one hundred well-filled large parchment pieces. The law report of the proceedings has survived although there are only brief mentions of the case in the national press. There were hearings on 25 January, 29 and 31 May, 16 December 1847, 13 and 24 January and 23 February 1848.

Put simply, the allegation against the members of the provisional committee were fraud, misrepresentation, and negligence (pretty comprehensive allegations.) Over thirty persons were sued including the Thompson father and son, Sir Ralph Pendlebury, and the solicitors Jones and Pugh. The court records show several defendants were abroad. This was a device to be out of the jurisdiction and therefore out of reach and we have seen another example of this. Most had separate legal representation. One George Lewis became bankrupt before August 1846.

We must at this stage learn a new word or perhaps more appropriately understand an old one. The word is DEMURRER. According to the *Oxford Dictionary*, it is defined as a noun:

> legal objection to relevance of opponent's point even if granted, which stays the action till relevance is settled; exception taken.

As is usual, the report sets out the facts as agreed to the court or as the court finds them. Bill is the Victorian way of saying claim. The Vice-Chancellor Sir J.L. Knight-Bruce heard the case and delivered the various judgements and commented,

> The Bill alleged various acts of misfeasance on the part of the directors, and, in particular, that they did not allot all the shares, although they had more than sufficient applications for them: and the bill prayed for a dissolution, accounts, payment of the liabilities of the company, and distribution of the surplus among the subscribers. Some of the Provisional committee-men, who were alleged by the bill to have applied for shares, but never to have paid any deposit or accepted them, demurred.

It is now that the failure of Jones and Pugh to be shareholders or promoters is seen to work to their advantage. They can plead they are only servants of the company and have no direct responsibility. These proceedings were designed to get at names who had money. Then you see them slipping away one by one.

There were two legal cases that were relevant to these cases that the parties had to wait to be determined. Then for the Thompsons, for example:

> It is doubtful whether the demurrer may not be sustainable, by reason of the absence from the record of the person called the Mayor of Macclesfield—at least, on the theory of the Plaintiff's Counsel. I do not, however forget, that in cases of fraud committed by several persons, some may generally be sued alone, without joining the rest.
>
> As to the three defendants, the two Thompsons and Sir Ralph Pendlebury, neither of them is alleged to have claimed an interest, and neither of them is alleged to be a shareholder. The bill, as I understand the matter, states allotments were made to them, and not accepted by them. They have paid nothing. It is said that they of the provisional committee, and affected by fraud, negligence and misrepresentation. As members of that committee, it is said that, in effect, they are charged as having received the money in question, by themselves or by their agents.
>
> It is said they are charged with so much fraud, so much misrepresentation, and so much negligence, as they ought to be answerable. It is however, a settled rule of pleading that a defendant is entitled to have alleged against him, distinctly the state of circumstances upon, in a bill, relief is sought against him. There is abundant authority." the case against them is not stated with distinctness and certainty, either as members of the Committee or as agents, with regard to the fraud, misrepresentation or negligence.
>
> The Demurrer must be allowed.

Tubal Cain Jones (what a splendid name), a Wrexham draper, was allotted one hundred shares and was a Sibson supporter. It was ruled that Sibson did not have identity of interest with him. Each allocation was deemed a separate contract.

The defendants one by one escaped the action until it became apparent it would not succeed. I believe that once the judge had held, he was only able to deal with Sibson's personal claim, the funding dried up and he could not continue.

There has survived a letter from Richard Thompson dated 7 March 1848 but we do not know to whom it is written but I believe it is Richard to John's solicitor, Allington Hughes. It alludes to the political situation of the day

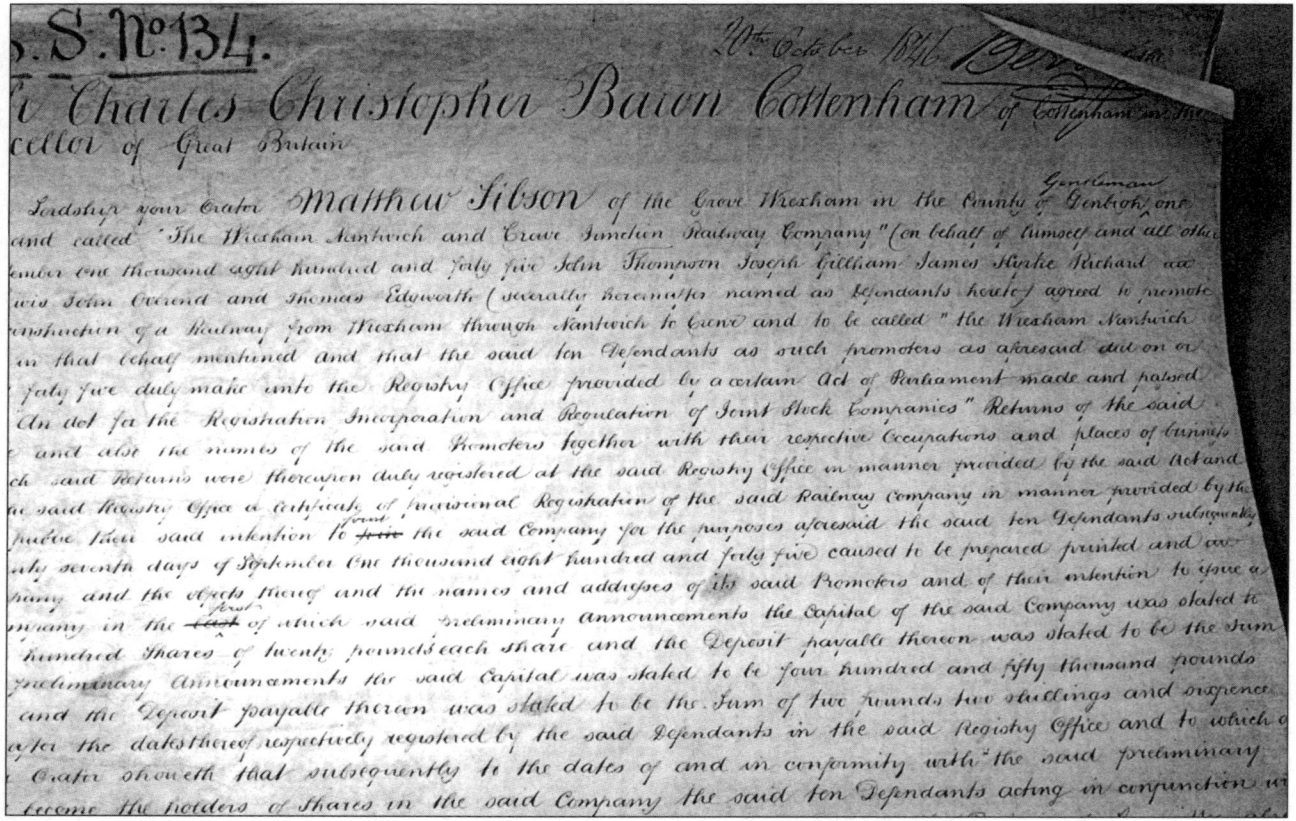

Face of legal pleading.

although it is about compensation for a bridge involving Roper. It is interesting in itself as it covers both local and international politics – Trevor-Roper's impending bankruptcy and Sibson's predicament after the loss of his court action.

> Has not the award respective the bridge been sent to you? The words of the award are that the Railway Company are bound to afford Mr Thompson proper access to the lands severed .We demand it. The sooner the better the money is obtained from the Railway Company for the land purchased from us.
>
> What must now be done with Mr Roper the sooner the better our hurts will be terminated with him for I fear like Louis Philippe he will soon have to abdicate for no doubt all his property must be sold. What is Mr Sibson doing with the directors of the Wrexham Nantwich and Crewe Railway I perceive his little schoolboys have presented him with some token of amusement to cheer him up.

There is an interesting postscript to this story. On Saturday 1 October 1853 there appeared a prospectus in the *North Wales Chronicle* for a new railway from Wrexham to Ruthin via Llanarmon and Rhydtalog. The acting Committee included none of those involved in the previous venture and support was expressed from some who had been involved before. One of these was Richard Thompson. Great claims were made for the line by the solicitors, Edgeworth and Pugh. The reader will not be surprised that the Wrexham public having been bitten before did not support the project and this line like that to Nantwich remains a figment in the sunset of the Victorian imagination.

The next major event is the coming of the Honourable Thomas Ffrench to Stansty Hall but that is another story.

Chapter 9
Mary Anne Thompson's wedding

When the Honourable Thomas Ffrench arrived at Stansty Hall, life would never be the same again. What do we know about his father's title that he was later to inherit? Charles Ffrench was created a baronet in 1779 and died in 1784. He had rendered services to the English Government but as a Catholic, he could not be seen to receive honours from them. His widow, Rose, was a Protestant and so in 1798, she received the title Baroness Ffrench of Castle Ffrench, County Galway (an Irish Peerage). It was clearly anticipated that the title would pass down the male line on her death. The second Baron shot himself in 1814 when his bank, Ffrench Bank, failed. His affairs were so chaotic that his will was not proved until 1915 some one hundred and one years later. Thomas was later the fourth Baron Ffrench.

But paternally he was descended from Sir Theophilus Ffrench who is said to have accompanied William the Conqueror to England. Originally they settled in Wexford but moved to Galway in about 1423. The ancestral home was Castle Ffrench which was of Georgian architecture in rolling parkland with twenty-nine rooms.

In 1851, he was forty years old and Mary Anne Thompson was twenty-three. How they came to meet is unclear but as an impoverished Irish Peer, it is not surprising that he should be looking for an English heiress to marry. But this may not be entirely fair. It was the custom of the time that the groom made a settlement in favour of the bride. This was to ensure she would never be penniless. We have no record of any marriage settlement in this case, but there is a record of a sale in June 1860 by Mary Anne Ffrench of lands of Carrowreagh and part of Barnoboy situate in the barony of Clare and County of Galway. It was a sale ordered by the Courts in Dublin at the request of Philip James Marjoribanks. This suggests that it may have been the marriage portion having to be sold to meet debts. There was always a shortfall while Lady Ffrench's father lived.

Castle Ffrench.

But the relationship of Richard Thompson and his son-in-law merits further examination. We know that there was no love lost between Lancashire Catholics and the Irish Catholics from the study of the question by Steele in the book on Lancashire Catholics, 'The English Catholics have always been the most bitter enemies of the Irish.'

There has survived an indenture of 26 February 1853 that is a conveyance to Richard Thompson of just over twenty-one acres of land by the Trevor-Ropers of Plas Teg. This land is located adjoining the old Mold Road and Wheatsheaf Lane in Gwersyllt. The price for this acreage is £1,675:00 and this is almost £70 per acre for one hundred years ago. The mines and minerals are excluded but Thompson clearly was enabled to work them through some other means or authority. Thomas Ffrench is made a party to the deed of the fifth part but did not need to sign the document.

The interest is in the declaration as to the Trusts on which Richard is to hold the land.

To have and to hold to the use 'of the said Richard Thompson and his assigns during his life and after the determination of that estate by forfeiture or otherwise in his lifetime to the use of the said Thomas Ffrench and his heirs during the life of the said Richard Thompson in trust for the said Richard Thompson and his assigns and after the determination of the estate hereinafter limited to the said Thomas Ffrench and his heirs during the life of the said Richard Thompson, his heirs and assigns for over to and for or upon no other trust or use trust interest or purpose whatsoever and the said Richard Thompson hereby declares that no woman shall become his widow and who but for this declaration would become servable out of the hereditaments and premises shall be servable thereout.

What does this mean? Richard seems to be saying you can have this when I am gone but not before and I intend to be around for a while yet.

The 1840s were a time of agitation in Ireland and at this time it was for the repeal of the Act of Union that had united both Parliaments. There were many meetings all over Ireland calling for repeal of the Act of Union.

Martin Ffrench Thomas' brother was in the thick of the movement as we find from the local Galway papers. The movement was the Loyal National Repeal Association and we find him in an open letter on 17 June 1845 urging the Association to accept his brother Jasper as a member and a letter from his father:

When Ireland shall have regained her place amongst the nations and that we shall participate in her honours as we now do in her humiliations, we shall point with triumphant pride as to an heir long-- to the undying honour which has been conferred upon us by the Loyal National Repeal Association.

Thomas appears more indolent than enthusiastic about repeal and adopts a more independent role (if you can say this of an Irishman). The Association meetings were well reported in the press and we find Lord Ffrench chairing a meeting in Galway reported in the *Nenagh Guardian*. Thomas is quoted speaking there:

It was his solemn and deliberate conviction that Ireland never would be regenerated through the medium of the Imperial Parliament, and that the restoration of her legislative independence was the only means to rise her to that position to which her population, capabilities, and her resources entitle her to hold. A population of nine millions was too great to be dragged at the tail of any other nation.

Clearly the man who came courting Mary Anne Thompson was an Irish patriot. But he had one saving grace. He was a Catholic. But the situation becomes more curious. The report in the *Wrexham Advertiser* of the wedding states:

although the intended marriage was only announced a few days previous to its taking place a most efficient committee was formed and immediate preparations made to mark the esteem in which the family are held, a public subscription was entered upon and a sufficient sum £80 was contributed to enable all claimants to participate in the festivities.

This would have been a major society wedding of the time. Mary's twin brother John James would have been expected to be the heir although he was not around. Time would have been needed for the bridal preparations. The Bishop of Beverley was there to perform the ceremony. But there is no evidence that any members of Thomas Ffrench's family were there. Why was there so much apparent haste?

Several possible explanations spring to mind. Mary was of full age and could marry without consent. She had inherited her father's wilfulness. The regime at Stansty was oppressive. We know in later years Richard thought his son-in-law was a spendthrift and a waster. He may well not have been enamoured with him at this early stage. If a date in the future had been fixed for the wedding would Mary still have been at Stansty on the day fixed. Would Richard have caused her to be elsewhere? Alternatively had Mary made it clear it was marriage now or an elopement. We shall never know. Her grandfather clearly had decided that he was going to enjoy the day. Richard paid up but was absent from all the various dinners held on the day to celebrate.

Richard provided twenty sheep for the festivities and the committee provided a fat bullock, that was distributed by ticket organised by James Mackenzie Kelly, the agent to the Estate. The town bells of Wrexham and Gresford and adjacent churches were rung. Triumphal arches had been thrown up across the streets and private houses decorated with laurel etc as far as the Wheatsheaf. The tenants were delighted about the wedding. Lord Ffrench scattered money after the ceremony.

Then the serious eating started. It is likely that the parties returned to the Hall. The Committee and friends adjourned to the Lion. In the evening another dinner was held at the Union Tavern after which the Committee went to the Turf to distribute the meat to those with tickets. Another was at the Talbot whilst the Frood Inn and the Wheatsheaf hosted two more. These were probably for John Thompson's key staff. The happy couple had left for London on the newly-opened Shrewsbury and Chester Railway at 4 p.m.

Mary Anne herself was clearly popular. So was her grandfather John. Thomas Edgeworth, who we have met before, chaired the dinner. He could be, as a lawyer, as obsequious as any other person. How much is true? But we can learn of Mary's popularity.

I augur the happiest issues from the union. Ireland is destined to be their future abode, and I regard as a happy circumstances the changes now taking place in that country, and I believe that when the lady in her own home, calls to remembrance the home of her childhood, and the happiness and prosperity which a judicious application of capital has diffused in the dwellings of the industrious poor there, that she would stimulate similar improvements in her own neighbourhood. I do hope that hers will be a happy future, and from the influence her high station and wealth will give, she will bear no small share in producing Ireland's regeneration.

We know from the chapter on the Department of Woods and Forests how Richard Thompson occupied common land and built houses on it knowing that in something like another twenty years, the Department might make him pay for the land. Let us see how Thomas Edgeworth describes his behaviour.

and the happiness and prosperity which a judicious application of capital has diffused in the dwellings of the industrious poor there.

That is not quite my interpretation of Chapter VII.

His tribute to John Thompson who was at the dinner is altogether as we know more accurate.

whose name was intimately associated with the prosperity of this neighbourhood, who for a much longer period than he could recollect had been a very large employer of labour and was equally appreciated as a good master and enterprising businessman. Mr Thompson had shown what might be effected by enterprise and skill on the most barren and unpromising land; he had not only succeeded in extracting from our mountains their mineral wealth, but made the turf produce turnips, and superseded the grig with grass. He is equally well respected in Lancashire. Go to Wigan and ask who is the most respected and revered man in that town and they will tell you it is our friend here. A man who, by his industry, his enterprise, and his skill has accumulated an ample fortune.

I have quoted at length from this speech and then its sincerity has to be thought about. When he replied, John Thompson was overcome by the occasion and what had been said.

for several minutes he was unable to proceed. Then he said the honour done to him was more than he deserved. Thirty-eight years ago he came to the neighbourhood and never regretted doing so. You are in a new country; the air is some of the purest in the world and the earth under your feet is teaming with riches. Capital enterprise, and skill, will eventually make this a most important district and no one wishes more ardently for its prosperity than myself. You must excuse me making a speech. I deeply feel my inability to thank you, in terms sufficiently warm, for your kindness to me and my family. But before sitting down, allow me to wish you all every temporal blessing.

A curious final phrase is that. We are told that a letter of apology had been received from Richard Thompson, not unusual in itself, but there are no records of his ever having attended such a function.

Fifty years later, a correspondent to the local paper, a James Ashley from Ewell in Surrey, writes nostalgically about his memory of the marriage when he had lived in Wrexham before he had moved away.

The place of Victorian women in society was poor and this was before the Married Womens Property Act started to give them some rights. Just under twelve months after her marriage, Lady Ffrench gave birth to her only surviving child Elinor, but her marriage was unhappy as we shall learn later.

But by any standards, this was some wedding and it is of interest to examine Richard's wealth.

Chapter 10
Richard Thompson – man of property

Although he described himself on his wedding certificate as 'Ironmaster', Richard Thompson's partnership with his father resulted in his not being directly involved in iron and coal soon after he had built his hall. They were clearly making a lot of money which enabled John Thompson to indulge in his love of horseracing and his son to acquire the land and build his hall.

John had clearly made sure that Richard knew the business that is why he operated his own foundry at Pant before his marriage. It seems clear that, after Richard Thompson had built Stansty Hall, his concern was, in modern parlance, a desire to build up his property portfolio. John was still very much at the hub of things and many purchases were within his sphere. It is noticeable that in the 1851 census Crispin Lodge, the house in the apex of the triangle that Richard Thompson enclosed, is occupied by one Edward Greenwood who is described as an 'ironmaster' and one wonders if he had anything to do with the Thompsons' industrial operations.

There is evidence of this degree of separation. On John's death, Richard WHO? was operating under a lease granted for forty years of coal from one David Francis Jones and, on John's death, there were still thirteen years left. It provided for the payment of rent and royalties. Richard went to John's solicitor Allington Hughes with this message that was set out in instructions seeking advice from Charles Blake Allmat, a barrister .

Mr Richard Thompson the son of the Lessee a gentleman of considerable fortune, irrespective of the real and personal estate which descended to him by the death and intestacy of his father, is very desirous in consequence of the state of his health of freeing himself from the responsibility and annoyance arising from the carrying on of an extensive colliery.

Advice was sought

whether he can by any act of his own under the lease void it by refusing to pay the rent and royalties within 30 days, by refusing to work the collieries, as he cannot now do so without the loss of at least 1/- a ton as the royalties do not amount to£150 a year? Is Mr Thompson bound by the covenant of his father to make it up to £150 or can he void the Lease by refusing to pay it or can Mr Thompson without the consent in writing of the Lessor assign the Lease and get rid of his liability?

In other words, he wanted nothing to do with the industrial operations. The advice which he received was clear and unequivocal, and he is told in October 1852

> He cannot avoid the Lease by refusing to pay the rent and royalties within thirty days in as much as clause 5 only provides that it should be lawful for the lessor to resume possession and immediately the term shall cease.
>
> I fear too that Mr Thompson cannot refuse to work the collieries under the covenant 7 as the words not leaving any coal cannel or ironstone ungot that can be possibly be gotten to advantage.
>
> It might be supposed that Mr Thompson, by breaking any of the covenants might avoid the Lease altogether, subject to an action for the breach. It has, however been held that a lessee cannot avail himself of his own act to vacate the Lease on the well known principle that a man shall not be permitted to take advantage of his own wrong.
>
> Had there been no assets of the late Mr Thompson, a question would have arisen as to the right of his administrators to waive the Lease, under the circumstances but I gather that the assets are considerable, it therefore appears useless to enter upon that question.
>
> Mr Thompson may as well try the effect of a request to the landlord to accept possession of the mines and Lease alleging the loss sustained by working.

In other words you are going to have to pay up to get out of the terms of the Lease. History does not tell us the terms, but I am sure it cost Richard Thompson a great deal of money. John had the drive to make the collieries pay, but Richard did not. In the end, he transfered both the colliery and the ironworks to the Sparrow family and to Poole who work them until the ironworks closed in 1903.

At his death, Richard held estate in land and property worth £200,000. By the time his daughter died in 1906, the value had dropped to £34,000, but this was still substantial. There had been few additions in her time. We have a catalogue of the properties that she owned at her death.

Public houses were a good investment in those days. Firstly there was the Wheatsheaf in Gwersyllt, with its own brew house and six acres of land, and the Tai (it was known by that name then as well) at Brymbo with another four acres. The Frood Inn had come up for auction in 1845 and John Thompson had tried to buy it then. It was known as the Racehorses, and perhaps this was part of the attraction for John Thompson. He failed to buy it and it was not until 1849 that he succeeded at a second auction. This is not the Ffrwd Hotel as we know it today on the road from Cefn-y-Bedd to Brymbo, but a much larger set of buildings at Windy Hill that was the focus of much of the area's social life after the chapels. It was described in the auction particulars as having two parlours and a large club room or function room for one hundred and twenty people, tap room back kitchen, cellars pantries and seven bedrooms stabling for ten and a cow house for twenty and other outbuildings including a very large room over the building. By the time of Lady Ffrench's death, the conversion of some of the buildings into cottages had taken place. The property is now a ruin but you can still identify its past glories. All three public houses were close to John Thompson's industrial operation. I believe that control of the men's social life would have been the motive for purchase

The remains of the former Frood Inn.

and not just profit. Drunken workmen do not work well and are a danger to themselves and indirectly to their wives and families.

As I have described elsewherehere, there were innumerable cottages built on land 'acquired' from the Department of Woods and Forests in Brymbo Minera, Gwersyllt, Stansty, Broughton and Adwyrclawdd.

We must not forget the 1500-acre estate in Ireland, Killoran, that was inherited by Ellen Thompson from her family. There is evidence that it was still in the ownership of Lady Ffrench in 1870.

Lady Ffrench also still owned eleven plots of land in Hope Street, after she had let the Roman Catholic Church have two plots (see Chapter XI). There was what is described as a capital house and brew house stable yard and conveniences in Hope Street. This is clearly another public house originally bought by John Thompson, but we do not know which. In 1855, Richard had sold land in Wrexham to extend the Militia barracks for £225 for a piece of ground 60 yards by 14. This land would be away from the Stansty estate itself. Bellan Farmhouse and land situate at Gwersyllt were also owned by her.

When Richard set out to build his hall he bought the two ancient manors or houses known as Stansty Ucha and Stansty Issa. Whenever land adjoining his came for sale he bought and so extended his land holding continuously. Stansty Issa is today much as it was then. Many papers relating to Richard Thompson's land transactions and those of his successors are deposited in the Wrexham Archives but they do not present a complete picture.

Stansty Ucha House was demolished by Richard Thompson as it was close to his new house, located on the top of the bank near Middle Lodge. It had also been known as Crispin Inn. St Crispin was the patron saint of cobblers and it is surprising how many cobblers lived in Stansty township, including Thomas Forgham, who lived in what is now known as Toll Bar cottage, the old gatehouse for the toll road. Palmer tells us that another house close by Crispin Inn was known as Crispianannia and he believed this name originated from John ap John of Stansty who was known as a cobbler and weaver.

Richard Thompson was constantly buying land and cottages in Brymbo, Coedpoeth and Minera. Poolmouth valley, the country park of today, was the industrial centre of much mining of coal. The records are littered with examples of transactions there. It is impossible to even hazard a guess as to how many dwellings Richard owned at his death but they undoubtedly ran into hundreds. The fields are named, but not the houses. John Thompson had bought much of the Frood valley and even acquired the remnants of the proposed canal and Canal House at the end of the 18th century. They bought as far as Cymau and it is noticeable that in 1875, the trustees of Richard's will were forced by court order to convey the minerals under Pentre'r-Fron Farm Wrexham (another litigious case for the Thompsons) to a third party. In Brymbo they even acquired ownership of the cattle pound and parish watering place.

The site of the Frood ironworks, with its two blast furnaces, offices, machine and machine house, blacksmith's shops and other buildings had been bought by John Thompson. Whilst they had leases of industrial sites they also owned much by way of land and houses that catered to a great extent for their workers. This wealth seems to have weighed Richard down and this, coupled with his family losses, led him into a life of seclusion followed by his death and the major court case regarding his will as we shall now learn.

Chapter 11
The will of Richard Thompson

When Ellen Thompson died on 21 November 1854, of what is described as 'English Cholera', caught it is believed when visiting the poor, the bottom fell out of Richard Thompson's world. An essentially very private man became even more so. In less than four years he had in effect lost his family. He became very vulnerable. Ellen was buried at St John's Church, Chester, where the legal if not the religious part of their marriage had taken place twenty-six years earlier. It seems clear that he had already decided she would come back to Wrexham to the church he would build. The St John's records show specifically that no funeral service was held there.

Even with the funds available to him, the building of a church was a major venture particularly as he was living at Weld Bank in Chorley after 1855. The church was built on land bought by him before Ellen died The foundation stone was laid on 9th May 1856, and amongst those present was Dr Killeen of Galway who was clearly representing the Ffrench family. Once it had been opened in 1857, his expenditure was not ended. Strangely, Richard was not present at the opening of the new church. He had built it in memory of Ellen in the belief they could both be together there. Her re-interment at St Mary's seems to have taken place only about two years before his death and again he was not present. His obituary in the *Advertizer* describes him as

> much respected amongst his own class for his modest and unassuming demeanour, and greatly beloved amongst the poor for his many acts of charity: one leading trait in his character being that the good he did in this way should not be known beyond the circle of the recipients thereof.

In June 1852, he had lost his father, John, with whom he had worked so closely for so many years. Nine months earlier, his only daughter, Mary Ann, had married her Irish peer and gone to live in the west of Ireland. There is a mystery surrounding his son, John James Thompson, from

STANSTY HALL, NEAR WREXHAM.

TO be LET, for a term of 14 or more years, and may be entered upon immediately, all that modern and commodious MANSION, called "Stansty Hall," replete with every convenience, and suitable for a family of the first distinction, with out offices, stables, coach house, harness room, clock room, fruit room, store rooms, milk house, cow houses, large sheep and cattle sheds, large tanks for the reception of rain and manure water, and every building necessary for a large establishment, shrubberies, walled gardens, pleasure grounds, and park land enclosed by high stone walls, with young and thriving plantations. the whole containing about 46 Acres of Land, in the parish of Wrexham, and county of Denbigh.

The Mansion contains lofty entrance and staircase halls, dining, drawing, music, and breakfast rooms, library, study, nine bed rooms, water closet, servants' hall, butler's pantry. kitchen and excellent wine cellars, a force pump, with excellent spring water for the use of the house kitchen, water closet, &c.

The garden walls are all wired, and well stocked with fruit trees of the choicest sorts ; the kitchen garden flats are also wired and planted with espaliers. Large Hot House, Conservatory, Pine and Melon Pits, Cucumber Frames, &c.

The hot house contains some of the finest vines in the kingdom, the fruit having for several years obtained prizes at the London Horticultural Society's Shows. The Hot House, Pine, and Melon Pits have just been reglazed with large squares of the best double strong crown glass.

The Mansion is situated on a gentle slope, about one mile from the Wrexham first-class Railway Station, commanding views of the surrounding country. finely wooded, and beautifully interspersed with gentlemen's seats. It adjoins the Wrexham and Mold turnpike road, having a handsome entrance lodge and magnificent gates, and is also approached by a back lodge with handsome gates.

The Wrexham postman calls at the lodge with and for letters every morning and evening

For further particulars, and to view the same, apply to Mr. KELLY, Henblas, near Wrexham.

Facing page: Advert for the lease of Stansty Hall.

Sales by Mr. Edisbury.

VERY

EXTENSIVE & IMPORTANT SALE

AT

STANSTY HALL,

Near Wrexham, Denbighshire,

On Friday and Saturday next, the 25th and 26th days of May,

To commence each day at 10 o'clock in the Forenoon, precisely

MR. EDISBURY has the pleasure of announcing that he has been honoured with instructions by RICHARD THOMPSON, Esq., (who is leaving the neighbourhood,) to offer for SALE BY AUCTION, upon the premises at STANSTY HALL, Wrexham, on the days above mentioned, the ELEGANT, SUBSTANTIAL, and USEFUL

HOUSEHOLD FURNITURE,

In DINING, DRAWING, and BEDROOM SUITES.

Superior Down and Goose Feather Beds, Hair Mattrasses, magnificent Pier and other Glasses with brilliant Plates, Brussels and other Carpets, choice Plate and Plated Articles, Brilliant-toned full sized cabinet PIANO-FORTE, six-and-a-half octaves, by "Broadwood and Sons," London; CHAMBER ORGAN; Splendid TELESCOPE, by Walker, on tripod stand, 44in. in length, with lenses, &c., complete in mahogany case, &c.

CARRIAGES, Kitchen and Culinary Utensils and other effects.

*** Descriptive CATALOGUES may be obtained at the principal Inns in Wrexham, Ruabon, Llangollen, Mold, Ruthin, Chester, Messrs. HUGHES & SON, Booksellers, or from the AUCTIONEER, Town Hill, Wrexham.

Advert for the sale of the contents at Stansty Hall.

whom it appears, he was estranged from about 1850. His son and heir was living in Brugge in Belgium and does not feature in the 1851 census. His death certificate throws a little light on the matter as the Mayor of Brugge registered his occupation as a *rentier* which is Flemish for a person who earns his living from property rental. The two informants of his death appear to be Englishmen of the same occupation although they are not related. The house where he died is a substantial one, but he could have been taken ill there. His address in England is given as Hillbank, Lancashire and this at least shows some line of communication with his father whose address it was. It has been suggested that he went to the Continent to train as a priest, but all the evidence suggests a different purpose entirely.

Richard Thompson, believing that Stansty had too many memories for him, decided to leave. He let the house on a fourteen-year lease and so did not intend to return. He sold virtually all the furniture and effects and went to live at Weld Bank in Chorley, in part of the Presbytery that had been the home of his uncle, the priest Richard Thompson, but which was then occupied by his cousin, the Reverend Henry Greenhalgh. The church in Wrexham was opened with much ceremony in 1857 and, althoughThompson was not there, one of the toasts at the dinner afterwards was to

> the health of their magnificent benefactor Richard Thompson Esq, the friend of the poor, the friend of every benevolent institution, whose hand and heart were ever open to every appeal.

In 1860, he paid for new organ for St Mary's from Gray and Davidson, the renowned organ manufacturers. Still he did not visit the church. There was one Wrexham man who kept in touch with him, his estate manager, James Mackenzie Kelly, a Scottish Catholic, who was forty in 1861. Kelly occupied Henblas, a large house near to Stansty Hall, as part of his remuneration. While he was seeing his employer the relationship seems stronger. Kelly swore an affidavit in 1867 (in connection with the will proceedings) which described Thompson's post Stansty life for us. The Scotsman had been the estate manager since 1844 and had married a lady sixteen years older than himself. It is interesting to see how the status of Kelly and his wife in Wrexham life becomes more significant – he and his wife were the guests of honour at the opening of the Stansty Ironworks at Gwersyllt and at the trial of a new blast furnace and a wide new furnace in 1865.

Henblas, the home of estate manager, James Mackenzie Kelly.

He tells the court:

> that for the last eleven years of his life the deceased (Richard Thompson) did not once visit his estate but left its entire control to me without any supervision whatsoever; That such Estate produces an average income of £2500 per annum and the arrears of rent unpaid at the present time (1867) do not amount to the sum of £100.
>
> That I possessed the entire confidence of the deceased who permitted me to receive his income to pay all outgoings and to apply the balance from time to time in payments to himself or as he may desire.

This affidavit was sworn as Lady French wished him to have control of the assets during litigation. Legally we call this Administrator Pendente Litem. Lady Ffrench in her affidavit describes her father's life at Weld Bank in these terms.

> [For] upwards of ten years before his death, he lived in strict retirement at Weld Bank Chorley in a small house adjoining or forming part of the

parochial residence of the Very Reverend Canon Greenhalgh Parish Priest of Weld Bank and for which house he paid to the said Canon Greenhalgh the annual rent of thirty pounds as I have heard and verily believe and during his residence at Weld Bank as aforesaid he did not spend more than the sum of three hundred pounds yearly upon his household expenses.

With respect to the furniture in the house occupied by the deceased at his death they are of inconsiderable value containing only one sitting-room two sleeping rooms and one or two servants departments as I have heard and believe.

We have this clear picture of Richard's very modest lifestyle for the last eleven years of his life. At his death, his estate was worth over £200,000. With his income and expenditure it is hard to understand why his bank overdraft stood at £8,000. Where was his money going?

Having settled his affairs in Wrexham Thompson's thoughts turned to the question of his will. If he had a will before Ellen's death its provisions would have been inappropriate. He had a son and heir who it would have been expected would inherit Stansty. His only other child is in Ireland and should be well provided for. His solicitor, John Yates of Liverpool, was consulted.

There was a clear rift between Thompson and his son. John had been in Belgium since about 1850 and one can only speculate why. He would appear to have received an allowance from his father but his other income is from renting out property. By 1850, under Queen Victoria's influence, Britain had become very moral. Was he co-habiting with a married woman and a Protestant at that? He was part of the English community there. Many British people transferred this type of behaviour to the Continent. It is unlikely we shall ever know the truth of the matter.

We know that Richard signed a will on 7 November 1855, but this was not his last. We have a full copy and it is pertinent and interesting to examine its contents.

He appointed Greenhalgh and the Reverend Edward Browne of Wrexham as his executors, giving them £100 each for their trouble. We then see the evidence of his estrangement from his son John James Thompson. He proposes to settle on him an annuity of £200. This at that time could be produced from capital of £6,000.

I devise to my trustees or trustee for the time being to stand seised of my real estate and out of one moiety thereof out of the rents of such moiety to pay to my son John James Thompson the clear annual sum of £200 until his decease or until he shall assign the same or commit any act or default whereby his interest in such annual sum would if it were to continue become vested in or transferred to his assignees in bankruptcy or insolvency in any other person or persons and I direct that this annual sum shall be paid by equal quarterly payments in every year so long as the same shall be payable the first of such payments to be made three calendar months next after my decease. This is unusual in itself but it gets more interesting as it goes on.

And as to the residue of the rents and profits of this moiety so long as the said annuity of £200 should be payable and as to the entirety of the rents and profits of this moiety in the case that the said annuity should cease to be payable during the life of my said son the trustees in their or his uncontrolled discretion think proper but not otherwise to pay the residue or the entirety as the case may be of the said rents and profits of the said moiety or any part of such residue in entirety unto my said son for his own use but the trustees shall in their or his absolute discretion as aforesaid at any time think proper not to pay the same or any part thereof to my said son then to pay the same or any part thereof if they shall think fit but not otherwise unto or for the separate use or for the maintenance of the wife and child or children of my said son for the time being or any of them or for the education or advancement of the said children or any of them in discharge of their or any of their expenses in such manner and in such proportions as the trustees or trustee shall approve and to accumulate any part of the said residue in entirety which shall remain unapplied for any of the said purposes expenses and the yearly produce of such accumulations to invest in any stocks funds shares or securities hereinbefore authorised for the investment of trust monies under this my will and with the like power to vary from time to time the said securities but so nevertheless that such period of accumulation shall not extend beyond 21 years from my death and shall stand possessed of this accumulation upon the trusts hereinbefore declared of the residue of the rents, profits of the said moiety and subject thereto upon trust for all or any the children or child of my son who being sons or a son shall attain the age of 21 years or being daughters or a daughter shall attain that age or previously marry and if more than one in equal shares.

On total failure, this fund was to be held as other half. Lady Ffrench's share was to be a life interest, paid for her sole use and benefit. Richard clearly did not like his son-in-law. The two only receive the income of half the estate and that also passes to their children as a life interest. On the failure of issue, the incumbent Roman Catholic bishop for the diocese in which Wrexham is located was to receive the residue absolutely.

Richard forgot the support he received from the Nonconformists when building the first Roman Catholic chapel in King Street. He was determined that no Protestant would inherit any of his money. He wrote that no person who had been

> brought up in or conform to the Protestant Religion in faith or become a member of any Protestant Church or shall abjure the Church of Rome then and in each and every such case the estate or estates hereinbefore limited to the person or persons who shall be so brought up in or conform to the Protestant Religion or faith or become a member of any Protestant church or abjure the Church of Rome shall immediately after his or her so being brought up to conforming becoming a member or abjuring cease determine and be void

This testament was in course of preparation before Richard Thompson left Stansty and such a condition as this became outlawed by the case of Clavering v Ellison, decided in February 1856. The law stayed one step ahead of Richard Thompson again. The will had been settled by counsel and was a very long document which had no appearance of being a temporary will until another was made.

However, the next will, that was the last was signed 4 June 1856. How was it different from the last one? The executors were the same. Thompson had taken out a life assurance for £2,000 on 21 January 1856 and, at his death, gave it personally to the bishop covering Wrexham. He gave his late wife's cousin, Bridget Mary Farrell, an annuity of £30 per year and his late wife's housekeeper, Margaret Williams, received an annuity of £20 per year.

The annuity of £200 per year is not included, but half the income goes to his son John and half to his daughter Mary, Lady Ffrench. The residue goes to the bishop if there is no surviving issue twenty one-years after his death. As the trusts are discretionary they are clearly designed to stop Lord Ffrench or any Protestant getting their hands on any capital, as he has had to drop his plans to bar non-Catholics inheriting. If a trustee died before Richard, or while the trust was operating, then the power of nominating a new trustee rested with Lady Ffrench.

But, on 8 May 1865, shortly before his death, Richard Thompson made a codicil to his will which fermented trouble. There were a spate of legacies, including an extra £20 a year for Margaret Williams and five other former servants. Kelly was appointed agent (at £140 per year) and given the occupancy of the Henblas whilst in the post and £30 for mourning for himself and his wife. There were certain specific legacies to Catholic Charities and to the Wrexham Infirmary.

Then the free hand being given to the executors became apparent. Greenhalgh and Browne were replaced as executors by two Catholic priests, Robert Wright Brundrit and Henry Hopkins. Brundrit was a convert in 1856 and then joined the priesthood. They do seem to have been of any special qualification but were perhaps chosen for their zeal. They were to have £100 each for their trouble. They could, without any limit on cost, fill the church with stained-glass windows at the free choice of the parish priest. They could also alter the furniture of the church, all the cost being born by the Stansty Hall estate. Certain building plots alongside the church building were given to the church, but they were not be used for burials or as a school site. He forgives any outstanding debts on the church.

He did think about his Stansty Hall estate that he had left ten years before and there was a clause in the codicil:

> I prohibit and forbid my executors and Trustees or any one of them or any other person or persons whatsoever to sink a pit or pits to get the mines and minerals under the land in the inside of my Stansty Hall Park Wall and that no pit or pits be sunk or mines or minerals begotten so as to do any damage or injury to the Farm Houses Buildings Walls Gardens and Plantations on my said property.

His son, John, died unmarried in 1864 and Richard himself died at Weld Bank on 5 May 1866.

Lord and Lady Ffrench were incensed by the terms of the will and codicil, and by the subsequent conduct of the executors over the funeral. They entered a caveat to prevent it being proved easily. When the executors tried to force the matter by warning the caveat, they filed a defence.

> 1. That the paper writing bearing date respectively the 4th June 1856 and 28th May 1865 and alleged by the Plaintiffs to be respectively the last will and testament and the codicil thereto of Richard Thompson formerly of Stansty Hall Wrexham in the County of Denbigh but late of Weld Bank Chorley in the County of Lancaster deceased were not duly executed according to the provisions of Victoria Chapter 6.

2. That at the time of the execution howsoever of the said Will and Codicil respectively the said deceased was not of sound mind, memory and understanding.

3. That the execution aforesaid of the said alleged Will and Codicil respectively was procured by the undue influence of the Right Reverend James Browne of Shrewsbury in the County of Salop the Reverend Henry Greenhalgh of Weld Bank aforesaid and the Reverend Edward Browne of Wrexham aforesaid or some or one of them.

There was evidence to support these allegations. When a will is challenged someone is appointed to look after the assets. Lady Ffrench was happy for the agent for the Stansty estate, James Mackenzie Kelly, to act but the executors would not accept Kelly as he had already been very critical of their behaviour. The affidavit that she swore expanded on this.

My Father, the said deceased, was during his lifetime and up to the time of his death, a person entirely free from ostentation and for upwards of ten years before his death lived in strict retirement at Weld Bank.

And did not expend more than the sum of three hundred pounds yearly on his household expenses.

The said funeral was conducted with so much state and ceremony that I am informed and believe that the expense thereof will not amount to less than six hundred pounds. I am advised that the enormous expenses incurred in the burial of my father were wholly unwarrantable and are not legally entitled to be paid out of the Estate.

The said James M. Kelly has informed me and which I believe, that prior to the funeral of my father he cautioned the Plaintiff the Reverend Robert Wright Brundrit against incurring unnecessary expense in relation thereto And the said John M Kelly has also informed me that immediately after the interment the said Robert Wright Brundrit applied to him as such Agent for money to defray such funeral expenses whereupon he gave him ninety pounds for the purpose.

The Plaintiffs in this cause, who are Roman Catholic Priests and claim to be Executors of my fathers will and codicil, who ordered the said funeral, were entire strangers to him having never seen nor had any communication with the deceased.

What was it, about the funeral arrangements, that offended Lord and Lady French and James Kelly so deeply?

Richard's body had lain at Weld Bank for a week to enable the poor to pay their respects. There were five mourning coaches for the journey to Wigan Station. Only three members of the family were there, his son-in-law and two Thompson nephews. These were his sister's eldest son and James, the son of his father's brother. The description of the funeral from the *Wrexham Advertizer* oozes expense. Entry to the church was by ticket only. There were thirty-two priests on duty, including two bishops. The costs incurred were clearly grossly excessive and were based on a belief that, with discretionary powers, they could expend the money in the estate as they liked.

There is no suggestion that Lady Ffrench was not in touch with her father after his removal to Weld Bank. But in her affidavit she admitted that she and her husband had lived the previous ten years in Ireland and complained, 'she was not made acquainted with the fact of her father's approaching death.'

We have to remember that Richard's views about his son-in-law were firmly entrenched and probably unprintable. Lord Ffrench had no difficulty in living beyond his means. The allegations made against the executors were such that any one of them could prevent the will being proved. The hearing in court was postponed by the bronchial illness of Lord Ffrench, but eventually took place in July 1867. Before the case was heard on 17 July, the parties had come to terms, but the report of that part of the public hearing as reported was interesting. The same report appeared in all the local papers.

> The testator was a Roman Catholic, and on the day on which the codicil was signed he asked two lads who had been serving at mass to witness the document Their evidence was positive, but Mr Chabot, the expert was called to suggest that from the appearance of the writing their statement was not true, and that Mr Thompson had signed the sheets of his codicil (a holograph document) as he had transcribed it, and had asked the boys afterwards to write their names on the paper.
>
> James Wilde said the Jury had rather a difficult task to perform, namely to decide between the positive evidence of the witnesses and the testimony of their own eyes as to the colour of the will.
>
> A juror. 'Is execution on a Sunday invalid, my lord?'
>
> 'O dear no.'
>
> A juror. 'Is a child of twelve years old a competent witness?'
>
> 'Yes.'
>
> James Wilde added that the difference between the colour of the ink was undoubtedly surprising, but it might have arisen from the use of blotting paper in one case and its non-use in another.

The jury deliberating for a short time found for the Executors.
The Court accordingly decreed probate of the Will and Codicil.

The legal need was for all (the testator and the two witnesses) to be together when they all signed. This case was in the very early days of forensic science evidence and it did appear likely that Mr Chabot was right. The terms of the codicil reflected what Richard Thompson had wanted on that particular day. But Lord and Lady Ffrench were infuriated in the way the press reported the case and this was the only issue decided. The report suggested that the Catholic priests, the executors, had won. But this was not the truth. Before the hearing terms had been agreed on 13 July.

The Catholic authorities had been desperate for a settlement and in January 1867 the help of Bishop Grant was sought:

> I am extremely obliged by all the trouble you are taking in the Thompson affair and I need not say how delighted I shall be if you can secure a peaceful solution of it. But Mr O'Neill is such a wild Irishman that I have not much hope of doing any good with him.

On 13 July, it was agreed that come what may the executors appointed in the will, and those appointed in the codicil, would retire and transfer the trusts to trustees nominated by Lord and Lady Ffrench, which finally took place in June 1868. But it did not stop there. The interest in the residue of the estate was surrendered by Bishop James Browne in a document dated 18 June 1868, after the two plots next to the church had been conveyed to them.

The press received a release in the following terms:

Brundrit and Hopkins v Lord and Lady Ffrench

Referring to a statement that recently appeared in this a paper respecting the trial of the case in connection with the Will and Codicil of the late Richard Thompson Esq, J.P. Stansty Hall, near Wrexham North Wales. We are authorised to state that by an arrangement entered into prior to the trial between the Plaintiffs who are executors and Trustees of the Will and Codicil and the defendants Lord and Lady Ffrench, the matters in controversy were reduced to the normal proof by the subscribing witnesses of the due execution of the Will and Codicil, and thereupon the Executors and Trustees and others were to renounce and Lady Ffrench to obtain administration from the Court of Probate which arrangement is now being carried into effect; whereby the deceased's Estates recently valued at £200,000 free from encumbrances, except a few legacies of trifling amount are now the property of Lady Ffrench the wife of the Right Honourable Lord Ffrench.

On 18 July 1868, Bishop Browne released his interest in the residue to Lady Ffrench.

It is perhaps ironic that Richard Thompson, who in his lifetime had been involved in so much litigation, even at his death should succeed once again and have one final involvement in the Court of Chancery! But for his daughter, Lady Ffrench, the stress and strain of these proceedings was to be surpassed by the personal struggle with her husband concerning the future of their daughter, Elinor, as we shall now learn.

Chapter 12

Lady Elinor Ffrench

Undoubtedly the saddest figure in this story is Lady Elinor Ffrench. She was baptized Elinor Marie Margaret Ffrench and was the only child of Lord and Lady Ffrench. She was born on 2 September 1852 at Ostend. Why her parents were in Ostend is unclear, but it suggests Elinor's arrival was premature. It is not an unnatural conclusion that Lady Ffrench had been visiting her twin brother in Brugge and was returning, via her mother's home, for the birth. It demonstrates the strength of the tie between twins that Mary Anne should visit her brother when heavily pregnant. It seems unlikely that Elinor was an only child by choice, as she could not succeed to the title. So Lord Ffrench was deprived of an heir to whom the title could descend.

Elinor would no doubt have received the traditional convent education but cannot have failed to be aware of the troubles between her parents. Divorce for the well-to-do had been introduced but was expensive. But her parents were Catholics and divorce was out of the question. Their relationship was turbulent and naturally Elinor was in the firing line.

It has been suggested that, when she was seventeen, a marriage was planned and she was not minded to co-operate and her parents ended up opposing each other in court. The case achieved notoriety and was widely reported. In February 1869, Elinor was placed by her father in the Loretto Convent, Rathfarnam, Dublin. The instructions were given to the Reverend Mother that she was to be kept there and her mother was to have no access to her. Lady Ffrench applied to the court for an order of *habeas corpus*. The proceedings were widely reported throughout Ireland and the United Kingdom. Once again a Thompson was in court.

The *Times* commented,

The little Convent case which sprouted prematurely here and promised to yield some seasonable gossip is likely to be nipped in the bud by being transplanted to the chilling atmosphere of the Court of Chancery.

This shows that enjoying a good story is not a modern attribute of our press, but this one stayed in public gaze!

On 10 February 1869, the *Belfast News-Letter* reported the proceedings before the Lord Chief Justice.

Mr Butt, QC, applied on behalf of Lady Ffrench who was at present residing at Calais for a writ of Habeas Corpus directed to the superiors of Loretto Convent Rathfarnam, to bring up her daughter who was at present detained in the school of the Convent.

Counsel moved on the affidavit of Lady Ffrench, which stated that her daughter was over sixteen years of age; that she had on several occasions expressed a wish to reside with deponent (her mother), but had been consigned to the convent by her father, from whom Lady Ffrench is now separated; that letters from Lady Ffrench to her daughter at the convent had been returned by the Lady Superioress, and all means of communication excluded from her. Counsel also read an affidavit filed by Mr Blaquire, Solicitor to her ladyship, in which he admitted having received a letter from Lady Ffrench on 22nd January last, for delivery to her daughter at the convent.

He accordingly went there on the same afternoon, and was received by a lady acting on behalf of Mistress Catherine Summers, the Superioress, who refused to hand the letter to the Honourable Miss Ffrench, stating as a reason for not doing so, that when the young lady was put into the convent her father gave strict injunction that no letter or communication was to be conveyed to her. He was aware of the fact that the young lady wished to join her mother some time ago when in England, and verily believed that she was now detained against her will.

The Lord Chief Justice granted the motion and made the writ returnable on Thursday next at 11o'clock.

Let us pause to consider what this report tells us. Lord Ffrench's decision to prevent his daughter receiving any communication from her mother is even by the standards of the time very harsh. Why was Lady Ffrench living in Calais and with whom? Could she not have used somewhere on her Stansty estate as a retreat? What account or story did Lord Ffrench give to the convent to secure their co-operation? It seems clear that the convent found itself drawn unwillingly into domestic strife that was not its concern. Lord

Ffrench was not by any standards being fair to his wife or his daughter.

We have open warfare between the husband and the wife and the problems are clearly very deep rooted. Lord Ffrench was clearly trying to use Elinor to get at her mother. At a time when a young woman needed the society of her mother, her father deliberately denied it to her.

But let us see what happened when the court re-convened a few days later. We have a variety of reports to choose from so let us look at the *Pall Mall Gazette* of 12 February 1869. We should also remember we are now in the days of the telegraph and messages can be passed very quickly.

THE IRISH CONVENT CASE

Yesterday was the day named by the Irish Court of Queen's Bench for the making of a return to the writ of *Habeas Corpus*, granted on the application of Lady Ffrench for the production of her daughter, a girl of sixteen now in the Loretto convent, Rathfarnam, where she had been placed by her father. Lord and Lady Ffrench had for some time been living apart.

Lady Ffrench complained that she was not allowed to see her daughter, and all means of communication were prevented between them by Miss Somers, the Lady Superior of the convent. Miss Somers was in court, but Miss Ffrench was not produced, an affidavit by Dr Cruise being tendered in proof that she was suffering from a severe attack of measles and bronchitis, was confined to bed, and could not leave her residence for a fortnight. Mr Butt Q.C. asserted that she was detained against her will, being in her seventeenth year. Counsel on the other side said a great many questions might arise in the case irrespective of the law. Mr Butt argued that there had been no submission to the court on the part of Lord Ffrench or the Lady Superior. Both parties were of the same religion, and there was no question of that sort involved in the case.

Up to the evening before Lady Ffrench knew nothing of the illness of her daughter. She was on her way from Calais to see her. The young lady was ill, and wanted the protection of her mother. Mr Butt added that she was now in the custody of parties who were detaining her in hostile hands.

Counsel opposing protested against the remark that she was in hostile hands. She was in a respectable school near Dublin. Mr Butt said it was so sworn, and her mother's letters had been returned to her. The Lord Chief Justice directed copies of the affidavits containing these statements to be served at the convent and on Lord Ffrench. Mr Butt further observed that Lady Ffrench's solicitor went to the young lady with an open letter from her mother, and the person acting for the lady superior refused to take it to the young lady. Finally, counsel for Lady Ffrench consented that if Miss Somers undertook that the mother should have access to the young lady the time for return to the writ should be extended a fortnight.

Why Lord Ffrench should have been so vindictive towards his wife is not clear and we are unlikely to ever know. It would be unwise to speculate as Lady Ffrench in her affidavit to the court expressly states that 'She is living apart from her husband, in consequence, she says, of family differences, in which she does not attribute any blame to Lord Ffrench.'

Freeman's Journal and the *Belfast News-Letter* in their reports quote the Lord Chief Justice's comments extensively.

The case is a very simple one. Sitting here in a court of law I have only, according to the law of *Habeas Corpus*, to see what is the inclination of the person said to be detained.'

'She is perfectly under the protection of the court at this moment. Every person who has knowledge of the writ is now under the authority of the court, and I would not allow the writ to be trifled with in the smallest particular without inflicting on all the parties who did so condign punishment.'

'Upon this motion I have some difficulty about making any order for access. It is natural that the mother should wish to see the child. If she applies and is refused I am here every day to listen to any application.'

'It's not very likely she will be refused.'

Mr Butt 'I am informed it's exceedingly likely my lord.'

'Let her apply for admission to see her daughter. If she is refused you can apply to me.'

Lord Ffrench, who missed this day's hearing because of bronchitis, was left in no doubt that the judge would not countenance any more prevarication.

A fortnight later we learn from the *Advertiser* that Lady Ffrench has seen her daughter and is satisfied that her illness is *bona fide*.

The final acts in this drama were recorded in *Freeman's Weekly* on 2 March 1869.

The Lord Chief Justice having stated that it would be necessary he should ask some questions of the Hon Miss Ffrench, would request all the parties to withdraw except Mr Nagle, Clerk of the court.

The counsel and solicitors on both sides having left the chamber, were recalled after a few minutes, and The Lord Chief Justice then said — 'I have had a conversation with the Hon Miss Ffrench, and she tells me it is her wish to go to her mother, and I have nothing to do but see her desire is complied with. Following the course adopted in a case before Lord Mansfield I now empower Mr Nagle Clerk of the Crown to conduct this lady to her mother, and I wish it to be understood that, exercising my power under this writ of *Habeas Corpus* if any person interfere with this lady's personal liberty I will consider that act a contempt of court, and immediately attach them.

Lady Ffrench is here.

Then let Mr Nagle conduct Miss Ffrench to her mother.'

Mr Nagle then conducted the Hon Miss Ffrench to Lady Ffrench who had her carriage waiting.

I wish I could say this story had a happy ending but, on 22 October 1870, Elinor died at Fitzwilliam Terrace, Bray of pleuro pneumonia at the age of eighteen years and her death was registered on 1 November. She was buried in the vaults of the cathedral in Marlborough, Dublin and, as the heiress to the Stansty estate created by her grandfather, Richard Thompson, with her death the line ceased.

In later years, Lord and Lady Ffrench declared a truce between them although it could not describe as a reconciliation. The society columns frequently recorded their movements from one house to another before Lord Ffrench died in 1892.

It is surprising that after the death of her daughter Lady Ffrench did not spend much more time at Stansty, the place of her childhood, but there is no evidence she was a regular visitor. In 1901, the head caretaker, John Malone, became the Stansty agent, and lived there with his daughter. He was Irish born, a tradition that covered the period of Lady Ffrench's ownership. He was the only person from Stansty present at her funeral in 1906.

We cannot trace any visits to Stansty by Lady Ffrench but we can learn about her Welsh estate in her absence.

Chapter 13
Lady Ffrench's Stansty

When Lord and Lady Ffrench regained control of the Stansty estate in July 1867 it was probably one of the happiest days of Mary Anne Ffrench's life. There had been a gross abuse of trust by the executors appointed on behalf of the Roman Catholic Church. The power given in the will 'should in their uncontrolled discretion think proper' had been interpreted by them as giving them a power not intended to apply for their own benefit ahead of the beneficiary.

It should be realized that, in accordance with the practice of the time, for large estates, an entail had been created by the will. This meant that only the income of the estate was payable to the heir. This prevented a dilettante heir in his twenties spending his inheritance and the capital was available for the next generation. When Charles Blayney Trevor-Roper was declared bankrupt, in debt to many people in about 1850, the Plas Teg estate was preserved for the next generation. In the case of Stansty, it meant that Lord Ffrench could not get at the capital, but they did need trustees who understood their obligations to the life tenant with the income of the estate.

So, at the instigation of Lord and Lady Ffrench, as a term of the settlement of the action on her father's estate, the trustees resigned and two others were appointed, namely the Reverend Robert Belaney and Henry Danvers Clarke.

Lady Ffrench's heir, Lady Elinor Ffrench, whose fate is dealt with elsewhere, died in 1870, and the Thompson line came to an end. By 1877, it was apparent legally that there would never be any more children and the entail was barred and full control of the estate passed to Lord and Lady Ffrench. This enabled money to be raised by means of a mortgage and £2,500 was borrowed from the West of England Fire & Life Assurance Company. A further £2,000 was borrowed in 1878 from Michael Charles Christopher Burke, followed by a further £3,000 in 1884. Life policies protected all the loans. These loans were raised to feed the inability of Lord Ffrench to live

Public Notices.

WHIT-MONDAY, 1896.

SHEPHERDS' —

DEMONSTRATION

ON STANSTY PARK, WREXHAM.

GREATER AND MORE EXPENSIVE ATTRAC-
TIONS THAN EVER.

HIGH-CLASS LONDON ARTISTES.

ACROBATIC CYCLISTS, AERIAL AND
HORIZONTAL BAR PERFORMANCES.

FOOT AND BICYCLE RACES:

120 Yards' Handicap, prizes value Five Guineas; 440
Yards' Handicap, prizes value Five Guineas; One Mile
Handicap, prizes value Five Guineas; Three Miles'
Handicap, prizes value Five Guineas; 300 Yards'
Youths, under 18, prizes value Three Guineas; 2
Miles' Bicycle Handicap, prizes value Three Guineas;
2 Miles' Bicycle Handicap (for those who have never
won a first prize), prizes value Three Guineas.

ENTRIE CLOSE TUESDAY NEXT. Forms can be
had from J. Taylor, Henblas Street, Wrexham.

DANCING. ' TWO BRASS BANDS. 5751

Advert for Whit Monday attractions at Stansty.

within his means. He died on 20 January 1892 and the loans were repaid.

We do not know how often Lady Ffrench visited her estates in Wrexham. She must have done or having a carriage with a carriage plate would have been pointless. She maintained a level of caretaking staff from the family's Irish estates.

During Richard Thompson's occupancy of Stansty Hall he maintained a level of personal privacy that resulted in the public at large enjoying no access to the lands. It was to secure this privacy that he had built the wall and got rid of the public road.

The new tenant, Thomas Irven, changed things. He competed in the local produce shows and in the professional section Strachan (later in business as Strachan & Evans and Mayor of Wrexham 1882), the Stansty gardener, regularly beat Erddig and Llwyn Onn in the professional section. In 1859, the *Wrexham Telegraph* said,

Amongst the flowers we noticed some rare and beautiful plants exhibited by Mr Irven. There were a number of very splendid geraniums, and fuschias, a remarkable fine cockscomb, and a grand show of dahlias, hollyhocks, etc. He had exhibited a beautiful specimen of Gesneria Zebrina a magnificent plant in full flower, to which the first prize was awarded.

But there is an amusing postscript to this story. The reporter was unhappy.

From some cause the reporters were not admitted into the tent during the time the judges were examining the specimens, so that we had no chance of getting detailed information, save in the midst of the throng and push of the public. Matters are arranged very differently elsewhere, such as at Chirk, where every accommodation and courtesy are shown to the reporters. In fact we ourselves were literally turned out of the tent, and our movements prescribed by the Police, on the pretence that our presence might interfere with the judges. This was a rather strange thing to say to us, when at the very time we saw the judges, three gentlemen who were also competitors, viz Messrs Bradshaw, E. Lovatt and McLevie. What right had they then, there on any pretence if even reporters were to be excluded?

We believe a dinner, a cold collation, or a something, was partaken of at the Turf Tavern, at four o'clock to which the reporters were not invited, the reason assigned being that the society could not afford it. Reporters are sometimes said to be like machines, and in this instance they were treated as such. They are expected to work to see everything and report everything, but are expected to want nothing, save perhaps a little water. We have even known them to be expected to notice and report speeches at entertainments when they had forgotten to invite them, and not only so, but to give a *rose de coleur* to everything.

In 1859, the gentlemen of the press thought they were entitled to special treatment. What has changed? Neither competitors nor members of the press corps would now be allowed to be present at any judging.

In 1855, Irven attended an Oddfellows meeting and was thanked for a

The carriage plate.

magnificent bunch of grapes he had given them. He attended a public meeting to express concern about the proximity of the new railway to Gwersyllt Church that he regularly supported.

This model of good citizenship had one failure when, in 1866, he tried to sue the Great Western Railway for the loss of his portmanteau and contents, and lost.

He had not been there much more than twelve months when the *Wrexhamite* tells us,

> [O]n the 29th August 1856 the children belonging to the Gwersyllt schools were invited to spend the afternoon in the grounds of Stansty Hall.
>
> After assembling at the schools at 2pm and dressed in their holiday attire they walked to Stansty with their teachers and preceded by the Stansty Band with their flags and banners waving. They were met by Mr and Mrs Irven, and a party of friends; who had been invited for the occasion. The children were then taken through the gardens, and seemed highly delighted with the beautiful array of plants and flowers which met their gaze in the hothouses and in the open ground. After perambulating the grounds they met at the Velles a point of the mansion that is tastefully and gorgeously decorated with flowers where they were abundantly regaled with tea plum cake and fruit. Grace was said before.

This becomes a major annual social event. In 1859, there were 265 children present and this had risen to nearly 300 by 1860. John Stevens (Stevens of Hope Street?) did the catering. The children were allowed to romp on the grass. The numbers had risen to over 550 by 1869.

Lady Ffrench initially had James Kelly to advise her and when the Hall was empty did not change the position. Although an absentee landlord, she was very interested in what was happening in Wrexham and to this day the first field on the right of the road leading from Ffrwd to Brymbo, after you cross the old Mold to Brymbo Railway line, is called Lady Ffrench's field by the older residents.

Her interest was demonstrated by a story that I learned but about which could not obtain independent verification. A Mr Evans, an Open University lecturer giving a local history lecture, knew about it. Apparently some time in the late 1860s, a man who had stock took them to graze on common land at Llanfynydd by Hope Mountain. He discovered the area had been fenced and so took the fence down and grazed his animals. He was apprehended and taken to Flint Gaol. He appealed to London against his sentence and Lady Ffrench took up his case by paying his legal fees. He was successful as the London court discovered that parliament, in authorising the enclosure, had not specified a penalty and he was released immediately. Some of the older residents of Llanfynydd can still identify the field in question. Some people might be unkind and say Lady Ffrench only took up the case because it was against the Trevor-Ropers of Plas Teg, who had won an action against her grandfather some years before, but I prefer to believe that she was atoning in some degree for her father's appropriation of common land twenty years earlier.

The farm at Stansty Issa passed in Richard Thompson's lifetime into the tenancy of a family named Griffiths (after whom the road at the rear of Stansty Issa is named). In 1854, we see the Denbighshire & Flintshire Agricultural Society gave the premium of £8 for the tenant and occupier of a farm, not having less than 100 acres, which was won by Mr Griffiths of Stansty. The description of his farming operations given in the adjudication is interesting in itself.

Mr Jas Griffiths of Stansty near Wrexham. This farm is held under Richard Thompson Esq, of Stansty Hall and contains 150 Acres. His crops consist of 23 acres of wheat, 18 acres of barley, 10 acres of oats, 17 acres of Swedes, mangold, and potatoes, 42 acres of permanent pasture, the remainder in one and two year old grass. It is cultivated in the five course rotation, 1st corn: 2nd green crops: 3rd barley and seeds: 4th grass, mowed and afterwards well manured: 5th pasture. Mr Griffiths has drained a considerable proportion of the farm, the landlord having found the pipes. He has also cut down and dressed all the fences on the farm, which were hedges planted on turf banks, with large open drains extending into the fields.

The banks are cut close and the drains filled up, and having an under drain, so that he can plough close to the fence. The fields are square, with fences which in a short time will be an ornament. Gates and roads good and well kept, and (setting aside his only being in the third year of his tenancy) the improvements pointed to me by the tenant, and confirmed by the landlord are very judicious.

After duly considering the merits of the different competitors for the premium both in regard to their mode of management, the state in which I found their farms; as to subdivision, fences, roads, gates, farmyards, buildings &c, &c I consider Mr James Griffiths justly entitled to your premium; and highly commend the other competitors.

We have to remember that his predecessor as tenant was Mrs Isaacs, whose husband John had committed suicide in 1845 and who had carried on with her son, John, as a helper. This is a very detailed description of the mid 19th-century farming in the Wrexham area and very illuminating. It also illustrates the nature of the ground Richard Thompson chose to enclose within his wall.

Lady Ffrench and her successor tenant James Griffiths's son, Thomas, also allowed communal use of Stansty. Originally the road we now know as Griffiths Road lead down from Summerhill towards the turnpike road but did not connect with it. It finished in the farmyard. It was probably during this tenancy that the final connection was made.

But Thomas Griffiths had a major fire in his outbuildings in 1885. The *Birmingham Daily Post* tells us all about it.

> The flames spread with such rapidity that, not withstanding the exertions of the Wrexham brigades and others, the whole of the farm buildings 70 yards in length, were gutted and the contents, consisting of oats, wheat, hay &, destroyed. Eight stacks of wheat, barley, and hay were also burnt, and the fire was not extinguished until an advanced hour. The tenant Mr Thomas Griffiths only finished harvesting on that day and the entire produce of the farm was destroyed. The damage is partly covered by insurance. The cause of the fire is unknown.

The rebuilt buildings are in place today.

In 1902, the tenancy was granted to Thomas Probert Griffiths – 132 acres at £549-15 rental. His relationship with Bishop Mostyn when he inherited is interesting. They were constantly in dispute over the terms of the tenancy and the interpretation of 'good husbandry.' There was no protection of tenure for a tenant farmer at this time.

Whit Monday was an important holiday. By the 1890s we were in the age when the friendly societies were in their hey day. One such was the Rose of Wrexham Lodge of the Loyal Order of Ancient Shepherds. Let us read from the *Advertizer* the report of the 1896 festivities.

> In the morning the members assembled at their clubhouse, the Albion Hotel, and were marched in processional order. They marched through the streets of the town in their full regalia, and carrying crooks decorated with flowers, and accompanied by two brass bands –the Wrexham Borough and the Rhos Brass Band.

The Griffiths children (Louise mounted, Annie on foot) in the rear yard at Stansty, c.1907.

Including juveniles there were about 250 in the procession, which formed an imposing sight. Stansty Park was the scene of the fete in the after noon, and as about noon the sun had shone out from behind the clouds, the entrances were besieged by crowds of people from the surrounding district, drawn thither by the natural beauties of the spot and in greater measure by the excellent programme of athletic sports, and other entertainments arranged by the fete committee. At about four o'clock there could not have been less than six thousand persons present, and the weather being beautifully fine, the number afterwards increased.

The entertainment provided was astonishing as well and their performance both amused and delighted the crowd:- Barton and Hart comedians: Prince Heyward ventriloquist, Mons le Blonde trapeze performer: Miss Jeanne, tight wire performer: Mons Raslus, somnambulist aerial performer: Bros Leoni, horizontal bar performers. During the afternoon the bands played selections, and dance music alternately with much acceptance.

This was the only event on in Wrexham that day. It was held very often at Stansty. It was an annual holiday and day out for very many people to enjoy. It was relaxation, but not all thought it so. We read from the *Manchester Guardian* of 21 October 1902,

AN ATHLETIC PRIZE WON IN A FALSE NAME
SENTENCE OF IMPRISONMENT

Yesterday, at the County Police Court, Wrexham, James Lucas Phillips, of Coleham, Shrewsbury, a well-known amateur runner, was charged with obtaining a silver-plated tea-urn, worth £4, by false pretences.

Mr Frank Kinsey, of Crewe, said on behalf of the Amateur Athletic Association of England, who governed most of the Athletic sports held in this country, on the 16th of August some sports under the rules of the Amateur Athletic Association were held in Stansty Park Among the entry forms sent in was one purporting to be signed by William Phillips, of Coleham, Shrewsbury, who entered the mile race, and received 125 yards start, the official handicapper believing him to be the defendant's brother, a novice. One of the lines on the entry form, in bold type read: "Furnishing false, misleading, or incomplete information will be a ground for disqualification, and will render the competitor liable to prosecution." Of course, had the handicapper known that W Phillips was in reality J.L. Phillips he would certainly not have given him 125 yards start, as he was only entitled by the rules of the Association to 85, and probably he would have had even less than that.

Mr C. Evans, secretary of the sports, said the defendant told him that he

Stansty Issa, 1911.

wanted to be penalised for having won a mile race a few days previously—
after his entry had been sent in. Witness said he would have to be penalised
14yards and defendant said that would be right. He was then placed on the
111 yards mark. He won the race very easily –simply ran away with it, in fact.
Mr H.P.Ellis, of Liverpool, the handicapper for the sports; the defendant's
brother, and others gave evidence in support of the charge. Mr Thomas
Maxfield Abraham, Crewe, vice-president of the Amateur Athletic
Association, said he received a letter from the defendant, in which he
expressed his sorrow for having run at Stansty Park in the name of his
brother. He asked that the Association would not prosecute him for the sake
of his wife and child, and promised to return the prize he had won. The
Association, however, could not accede to this appeal, as there was great need
of such prosecutions, when defaulting runners were found out, to prevent
others indulging in similar practices.

The Chairman of the Bench (General S.Mostyn) said the defendant had
been guilty of a very dishonest proceeding, and he would have to go to prison
for one month with hard labour. The Court had dealt with him as leniently
as they could.

Clearly, cheating in any sport is not a modern innovation. It showed the
importance attached to such sports on a family day out by the controlling
authorities and Stansty played its part.

The 1891 census shows Lady Ffrench's coachman, born in Wrexham,
living in the Top Lodge. But we do have to remember that Lady Ffrench was
a Thompson through and through so it comes as no surprise to read in
Freeman's Journal for 3 July 1896 that she was being sued for an unpaid debt.
The case ended up in the Court of Appeal where she was sued by a person
named Wood for £93-19-6 for professional services and goods. Judgement
was given against her for £33-10 with costs. When the taxing master taxed
the bill he did so at a higher scale. The Court of Appeal reduced the scale.

Lady Ffrench's roots were Wigan and Wrexham so it is interesting to learn
how Irish she had become. The *Manchester Guardian* reported that on 28
December 1903, Lady Ffrench gave £1,000 for the erection of a high altar in St
Joseph's Oratory on Highgate Hill, London, on condition that all the materials
utilised in its construction were of Irish origin.

We must move on to ascertain how Stansty was affected by her death.

Chapter 14
Bishop Mostyn's Stansty

After the death of Lord Ffrench at Elm Park Dublin in 1892, from influenza and bronchitis, Mary Anne Ffrench was very much on her own. Her husband had been a Deputy Lieutenant for Galway and a Justice of the Peace. She had no family of her own and the title had passed to her husband's brother who was very much an Irish-based Irishman. It is true that she still figured in Dublin society, but of course as the Dowager Lady Ffrench. She attended a reception for Queen Victoria in Dublin in 1900. She lived in Merron Park in Dublin as, having been away for over forty years, she has no close friends in North Wales.

But events were happening at Wrexham that would prove significant over a period of time. It was decided by the Roman Catholic hierarchy that there will be a re-organisation of the Church that will affect the town. The town will become the focus of a new diocese, to be known as Minevia, and Richard Thompson's church will become the cathedral for that new diocese. At this stage, St Mary's was a fairly dull Victorian building of the solid, mid Victorian architect Pugin the younger. The choice of being the first bishop of Minevia was given to a North Wales man, Francis Mostyn, the brother of Sir Pyers Mostyn from Mostyn Hall in Flintshire. The pen portrait in the *North Wales Guardian* on the occasion of his consecration, deals with the secular aspects of his character that will be shown to interest us later. He is described as,

young, handsome and full of vigour and speaking in his native tongue, his career will be watched with interest.

He was distinguished for the fine vocal and dramatic powers, and in the choir and on the boards he won unstinted admiration. He excelled in all manly sports-cricket, football, swimming, fishing, or following the hounds on foot were favourite pursuits wherein he was second to none; and even at the billiard table in the common room he hardly found a match. He was a fine shot and retained his interest in cricket. His personal relations were marked

---

Stansty Issa when used as the clubhouse for Wrexham Golf Club.

by a cheerful friendliness. Was incapable of any surprise at any vagary of human conduct.

He had all the qualities that any person who would befriend Lady Ffrench would require.

He was appointed curate under his cousin Monsignor Slaughter at St Mary's Birkenhead.

The name Slaughter also plays a significant part in this story.

Bishop Mostyn found the daughter of the builder of his cathedral adrift from the church in Wrexham after the affair of the will in 1867 and sets out to repair bridges. Initially, Monsignor Slaughter, who has been overtaken in the hierarchy, went to see Lady Ffrench in Dublin in 1896. Bishop Mostyn soon followed and he was very personable to the lonely Lady Ffrench. By the time of her death after a lingering illness on 3 June 1906, he had been a regular visitor to her. When she fell ill he led prayers for her during the confirmation service in Wrexham on Whit Sunday and we can read in the *Wrexham Guardian* that he had only just returned from a visit to her in Dublin when he had to return immediately to Ireland on hearing of her death. He conducted her funeral.

Lady Ffrench's will, prepared by a prominent London firm of solicitors

Slaughter & May, was read and the firm's senior partner, Slaughter, was appointed as one of the two executors. In it, she leaves her friend, Francis Mostyn, after a few minor bequests, her entire estate. The mistake, of appointing priests as the executors that had created the problems over her father's will was avoided, but nothing is ever simple in the case of a Thompson will.

Ellen Margaret Ormiston, described as a cousin and heir-at-law, entered a caveat to prevent the will being admitted to probate. Who is she? She was born in 1876 and was married at St Georges Hanover Square to Ormiston and elected to take as her married name her own surname added to her husband's. She was therefore known as Fitzadam-Ormiston. Her father was John Thompson Fitzadam who had married late in life Mary Murray Wood of Fife in Scotland. Her father was Recorder of Wigan and died aged 62 when she was ten years old and an only child. Her father had followed his father Adam Fitzadam as Recorder of Wigan and he had been appointed to the office in 1828. This is significant as he must have been a Protestant as this was before Catholic Emancipation.

Adam Fitzadam married by special license Ellen Thompson, the daughter of John Thompson, at All Saints Church of England Church, Wigan on 27 December 1821. She was Richard's elder sister, having been born in 1797, and John Thompson Fitzadam's mother. We have an interesting parallel with her niece. We have already heard of the haste of Mary Anne to be wed. The special license for her Aunt Ellen is dated 26 December, the day before the wedding. It does appear that when a Thompson girl decided to marry she did not hang about for any complicated proceedings or wedding preparations. She died at Clevedon near Bath on 21 August 1873. There is no record of any marriage service in St Mary's Catholic Chapel, the Thompson place of family worship and the marriage promotes much conjecture.

She was of full age and, as with all Thompsons, knew her own mind. I have no doubt she married Adam Fitzadam against the declared wishes of both her brother and her uncle, Richard. Was it her Protestant children that Richard in his pre-1855 will was trying to protect his estate from? On the other hand, her father's tolerance was such that he enjoyed a good relationship with his Protestant grandchildren, working particularly closely with John Thompson Fitzadam on Wigan Borough Council. Fitzadam refused to become an alderman on John's death in 1852, I believe on the grounds of unworthiness. How is it therefore that she was allowed by the Thompson

Stansty Hall in Mostyn's time.

family to marry a Protestant?

It is surprising how often 'Ellen' appears in this story as a Christian name. Ellen Margaret Fitzadam-Ormiston's relationship is that of second cousin. So Lady Ffrench's Irish cousins were three times removed. Ellen Bourke was an only child (as described in the report of Richard's marriage) whilst Richard Thompson is described as an only son.

At Lady Ffrench's funeral in Dublin the *Irish Times* tells us that there were three Blakes present. They are described as cousins and are clearly on the Irish side. It is also very clear how supportive the remaining Ffrench family were. The *Times* waxes lyrical about Lady Ffrench.

> Her demise has caused widespread grief amongst the poor of the neighbourhood. The free and ready help Lady Ffrench gave to every charitable cause made her name widely known as a benefactress and a helper to everyone in distress, and her loss will be felt keenly by all who knew her.

But an administrator *pendite litem* was appointed, Ernest Layton-Bennett, a chartered accountant. We learn from the *Times* on 13 November 1906 that the defendant's solicitors had written saying that their client's definite and final instructions were not to proceed further with the case. As, however, the estate was a substantial one, amounting to £34,215 gross (of which £23,810 was realty), it was necessary to obtain proof in a solemn form. The rents from the estate were £2,500 per year. Additionally, Lady Ffrench had horses, carriages, furniture and jewellery.

Evidence having been given in support of the will and codicil, Mr Justice Bargrave Deans pronounced for the executors. Mr Murphy appearing for the executors asked for costs against Ormiston to include several sums that the judge granted. Ellen Margaret Ormiston then decided to discontinue her opposition and we have no idea why.

There is no doubt that she and her husband were already well off. It could have been a lack of funds, or an evaluation of her chances of upsetting a will prepared by a solicitor who was at arm's length. Another grant of probate was made to the original executors The Right Honourable Arthur Robert Pyers, Viscount Southwell, and William Edward Slaughter on 30 November 1906. The value of the Estate was then £37,229-7-5. The executor was the brother of Monsignor Slaughter.

And so the residue of Richard Thompson's Welsh estate was inherited by Francis Mostyn, the second time a member of the Mostyn family has been involved with Stansty.

During Lady Ffrench's lifetime, a lease had been granted of the Stansty parkland to the Wrexham Golf Club Limited of which Francis Mostyn was the President. The Golf Club land was later sold by Bishop Mostyn to the Golf Club after the death of Lady Ffrench.

At this stage, we must remember that the church built by Richard Thompson was very plain. So Bishop Mostyn decided to use his inheritance to improve it, particularly by the installation of stained-glass windows. He clearly did not have any feelings for Stansty as an estate and started to dismember it. He sold the main gates that were of special intrest to Simon Yorke of Erddig Hall who had clearly coveted them for some time (see chapter 6).

Richard Thompson had left money under his will to establish the Stations of the Cross, but these were not completed until 1906. Could Lady Ffrench be encouraged to pay for some stained-glass windows? To this end she was courted from 1896 and behind the Bishops Chair is a rose formation (ten windows in all) with the inscription,

This window was erected by the Right Honourable Lady Ffrench in memory of her husband the Right Honourable Thomas, 4th Baron Ffrench, who died 19th December 1892.

Two other windows, dedicated to Lord and Lady Ffrench, were installed, both to Saints Anne and Teresa. With her difficult marriage history Lady Ffrench put the memorial in Wrexham rather than Dublin where they were both interred (as also was Elinor Ffrench). After the issues of 1867 it is difficult to imagine Lord Ffrench supporting this decision had he had a say in the matter. Bishop Mostyn's inheritance certainly helped in his plans for beatifying his cathedral. From 1908, Father Quinn, on behalf of the Wrexham Cathedral, was in touch with Hardman's, a Birmingham firm leading stained-glass window designers.

While it is necessary to recognise the effects of the Great War on the financial state of the country, there is so much evidence of neglect by Bishop Mostyn during his ownership of Stansty. Fortunately, after the return of peace, there appeared on the scene Henry Dyke Dennis of New Hall Ruabon, who saw Stansty as an appropriate home for his son and he was prepared to spend money to put it right.

Chapter 15
Post Mostyn Stansty

After the neglect following the death of Lady Ffrench in 1906 and the travails of the Great War, when Army occupation damaged the house that Richard Thompson had built, Stansty found an owner who wanted to appreciate the estate for itself.

Henry Dyke Dennis the son of Henry Dennis from whom he inherited very extensive industrial interests. In 1909, he bought Stansty Issa or Stansty Farm and a further 104 acres from Bishop Mostyn. At that time it was being farmed by Thomas Probert Griffiths a local Nonconformist some of whose descendants now live near Denbigh and who have been referred to earlier. He had inherited the tenancy of the farm and Griffiths Road that divides the Boozey Field from the main house was clearly named after him. It was only the house and garden and the land, although adjoining, was outside Richard Thompson's wall.

I should pause here to explain the name Boozey. It was a name on this field when our family came to Stansty in 1953. For very many years, we believed that the name had come from some alcoholic occasion held there at sometime in the past. But the explanation is much more interesting. Boozey is the name for the evergreen Christmas decorations, other than yew, that were fed to the cattle after Christmas in the field behind the house. That is where the Boozey field is located, behind Stansty Issa or Stansty Park.

Dennis required possession and the Griffiths family moved out. The house was used for a while as the clubhouse for the Wrexham Golf Club that was based there with a nine-hole course at that time. Then, in 1912, Dennis bought the pool or lake in front of the house and the glade alongside it containing just over an acre. There is a limit on the water level for the lake. It was probably Dennis who planted hundreds of crocus and daffodils in the glade. The war intervened and in about 1924 the golf club moved out to its present home at Borras and on 1 January 1924, Dennis bought the vacated golf course and all the buildings (including the two lodges and the stables house) within Richard Thompson's wall. All this was in front of Stansty Issa.

I believe that it was Dyke Dennis who demolished the Stansty Hall built by Thompson and which was finally ruined by the war. There is evidence of his warming to restoring the Stansty created by David Edwards. The portico seen on all the old photographs of the hall was dismantled and re-erected alongside Stansty Issa, now known as Stansty Park. Part of the hall remains and was converted into a home by my late father. Dennis also brought many of the ornaments from the hall garden . He laid out the rose garden and the herbaceous border and Italian garden. He planted very many fruit trees. The holding of land with the house steadily increased. Work was done to convert the pond into an ornamental pond or lake. There were several very large stone troughs that were put into their present position by my father which enhance the garden and must have been brought down by Dennis from the hall at the time of demolition.

The lodges were brought up to standard and Stansty found its soul again. The Top Lodge, on the Summerhill road, illustrates this. A tree fell on this lodge in the late 1920s, breaking through the roof. Because of this, Top Lodge is the only building at Stansty that does not have a slate roof as Dennis replaced it with tiles he had manufactured.

Troughs.

All that is left of Stansty Hall today.

Stansty became a place where racehorses were trained and John Thompson would have approved. The gallops were on the Gwersyllt side of the mineral railway, but the stabling was in the middle of the land in front of the house, and had been the stables of the old hall. Victor Dyke Dennis, Henry's son, lived at Stansty Issa (or Stansty Park as it is now known). He trained horses for his father, mainly steeplechasers. There was a steeplechaser named Stansty that ran regularly but its best, so far as I could trace, was to finish second, but as it was usually last I wonder if the other horses had fallen. A large agricultural unit was created which included Plas Coch, which years before had been occupied by the Merediths cousins of the Edwards.

Dennis also farmed and the milking herd was based at Plas Coch whilst the fodder was grown on the Stansty land. The estate had chickens and a beef yard. The Boosey field was used for mares and foals. The stable boys were usually Irish and were housed in the Plas Coch Cottages after the death of the waggoner. Stansty had only two cows to milk for the house.

When Dennis sold in 1946, the farm bailiff was one Jack Cliffe. He had taken a tenancy of Pandy Farm and at the dispersal sale of the livestock he bought five of the best milking cows as he of course knew the animals very well. Five others then helped him to drive the cows he had bought along the roads, under the bridge by the Walnut Inn to Pandy. Imagine the chaos if cows were driven along this route today.

I have been given a picture of life at Stansty by Anne Gray whose aunt, Nancy Thomas, was employed by Victor Dennis as a nursery nurse to look after master Jeremy Dennis and his sister Susan, who were both older than her. When she was about four, in about 1942, she was invited to tea with the children. They had formal tea in the middle of the front lawn on a table and she has this lasting memory of their genteel living. There were ducks on the lake which she remembers feeding with her pickled onion as she had never had one before. She was given a little basket about three-inches square with beads and a little doll to go home with.

Dennis owned Gresford Colliery at the time of the disaster and when we arrived at Stansty in 1953 the electricity supply still came from the colliery.

Stansty then passed to Thomas Corrie whose ancestors came from Park Hall, Oswestry. He owned a Lagonda that he used if he wished to impress and a Hillman Minx shooting brake the rest of the time. He held much of the land previously held by Dennis, including the two farms. He trained racehorses there until 1953. He then moved as he felt he had not enough room. Mrs Corrie had been very interested in the garden and was very keen on her gardeners weeding the crazy paving. Clearly she fostered the garden that was in very good shape when our family took over in 1953.

It was my father's intention to have a dairy farm and he established a herd of pedigree dairy shorthorns. He bought cows from the Duke of Westminster to establish the herd. There was already a Stansty herd registered so it was called Stanpark.

The newly re-formed Wrexham and District Sheepdog Trial Society asked to hold their sheepdog trials at Stansty and they were there a few years before the society folded because of the lack of support from the public. There is no finer sight than to see a group of sheep under the control of the shepherd and his dog being brought down from the top corner of the Park and penned.

Besides building the wall, Richard Thompson had planted very many trees which are such an attractive feature of the layout that they are all subject to Tree Preservation Orders. All British trees are represented including oak, ash, beech, sycamore, horse chestnut. There were once many elms but these were decimated by Dutch elm disease. We have probably planted as many if not more tress than Richard Thompson and the stage is now arising when

The view looking towards the site of Stansty Hall.

his trees are coming to the end of their natural life and our planting is effectively replacing them.

Stansty is its own entity. It commands loyalty. David Edwards' staircase remains the challenge I had to go up without my light-sleeping mother hearing me! The noise of modern-day traffic cannot prevent an appreciation of what life and views were enjoyed in Thompson's own time. The hares that were present when we arrived have been replaced by too many rabbits. Modern agriculture requires too many acres. Stansty has become an oasis between Wrexham and Gwersyllt. Its personality remains to be enjoyed by future generations.